86 Treatment Ideas & Practical Strategies

for the Therapeutic Toolbox

JUDITH A. BELMONT, M.S.

PESI®

Eau Claire, Wisconsin

2006

PESI, LLC
PO Box 1000
200 Spring Street
Eau Claire, Wisconsin 54702

Printed in the United States of America

ISBN: 0-9749711-9

PESI, LLC strives to obtain knowledgeable authors and faculty for its publications and seminars. The clinical recommendations contained herein are the result of extensive author research and review. Obviously, any recommendations for patient care must be held up against individual circumstances at hand. To the best of our knowledge any recommendations included by the author or faculty reflect currently accepted practice. However, these recommendations cannot be considered universal and complete. The authors and publisher repudiate any responsibility for unfavorable effects that result from information, recommendations, unde-tected omissions or errors. Professionals using this publication should research other original sources of authority as well.

For information on this and other PESI manuals and
audio recordings, please call 800-843-7763 or
visit our website at www.pesi.com

SAM011335

ACKNOWLEDGMENTS

This book was inspired by the clients and workshop participants throughout the years who have let me into their lives and given me the opportunity to learn so much. I am particularly indebted to one of my very first jobs, the "Why Not" program in Worcester MA, as this program laid the foundation for me to pursue my passion in promoting "hands-on" mental wellness education. Later on, The Center for Humanistic Change in Bath, PA, furthered my knowledge and expertise in this area. Both places laid the foundation and offered the creative tools and mindset that have served as a base and inspiration for my work. Thanks to Michael Olson from PESI who has spurred my interest in writing this therapeutic guide. Special thanks above all to my husband, Don, and three wonderful sons, Justin, Brian, and Adam, who have been the best supports, teachers, and guides of all!

TABLE OF CONTENTS

INTRODUCTION

The challenge of therapeutic intervention is to help facilitate change. Some clients see counseling as something that "works" or "doesn't work." This workbook helps clients take a proactive approach to the therapeutic process. Through use of experiential activities, exercises, self-help worksheets, and educational handouts, individuals can experience change—not just talk about it. Even for the most treatment-resistant client, these T.I.P.S. for your therapeutic toolbox can be life altering.

Why is it often so difficult for people to change? Therapeutic intervention all too often relies on one modality of intervention—talking. Words accompanied by experiential learning can reap benefits exponentially. Creative media tools can unleash powerful insights where talk therapy leaves off. The power of cinematherapy and bibliotherapy hardly have scratched the surface of their potential impact on psychological intervention. Additionally, because so many clients experience decreased short-term memory, confusion, and lack of attentiveness when in crisis, clearly written handouts can aid in reinforcement of learning.

Even with the most treatment-resistant individuals—especially those with characterological issues—tips and tools can teach skills that might break through treatment-resistant features. With experiential, interactive exercises, even the most strongly erected defenses are broken through.

As Confucius said so aptly, "Teach me and I will forget, show me and I will remember, involve me and I will understand."

This book is designed to help all types of mental health practitioners or those who conduct "mental fitness / mental wellness" workshops and trainings. These 86 tools and T.I.P.S. augment more traditional forms of psychological treatment. Unfortunately, life skills training is rarely a part of formal education, and this workbook attempts to help people learn basic life skills not taught in schools.

This book is designed to be "user friendly"—easy to read and understand, for immediate implementation into your therapeutic practices. My mission is to increase mental health and mental fitness, whether it be in clinical practice, hospitals, outpatient clinics, prisons, residential treatment facilities, or the workplace. I also apply these activities to my work in the corporate setting through Worksite Insights™. These T.I.P.S. and tools are designed to enhance the therapeutic experience in any setting by facilitating growth and healing through education, insight, active participation, and involvement.

These 86 "Therapeutic Ideas & Practical Strategies" are broken down further into "working" T.I.P.s for each activity, handout, or strategy. Each T.I.P. is broken down into Theory, Implementation, and Processing—hence the acronym "T.I.P."

The handouts and worksheets in this book can be copied for personal use in working with individuals or groups. If there is interest in using any of these T.I.P.S. in any type of publication, it is required that permission be granted by the publisher.

QUOTES FOR GETTING ORGANIZED

"For every minute spent in organizing, an hour is earned."

—Unknown

* * *

"Organizing is what you do before you do something, so that when you do it, it is not all mixed up."

—A. A. Milne

* * *

"There is in the act of preparing, the moment you start caring."

—Winston Churchill

* * *

"Information is a source of learning. But unless it is organized, processed, and available to the right people in a format for decision making, it is a burden, not a benefit."

—William Pollard (CEO, Servicemaster)

Getting Organized

T.I.P. #1
GETTING ORGANIZED WITH A FOLDER FOR CLIENTS

THEORY: Therapeutic interventions involving practical "hands on" methods are vital to the therapeutic process. To bring therapeutic effectiveness to a heightened level, the use of experiential exercises, handouts, worksheets, "self-help assignments," and activities offer infinite possibilities. This workbook offers many ideas to use in everyday practice, in all therapeutic settings, with individuals and groups. They are versatile and readily adapted by mental health professionals working with all types of populations who could benefit from developing skills for living—that is, each and every client!

IMPLEMENTATION: Since many of the activities and ideas are in the form of handouts, each individual can benefit from having a folder to keep all materials in one place. A 2-sided pocket folder would be fine, as would a small binder where clients can keep handouts organized. I have found this method helpful in limiting the chance of clients losing handouts! You either can put a label on the folder (e.g., name and title such as "self-help assignments") or have clients make up their own titles to reflect what this process means to them.

PROCESSING: Explain to clients the importance of "self-help assignments" as a means to keeping them responsible for their own growth and wellness. Differentiate between the concept of "homework" and self-help assignments. The former often is viewed as imposed from the outside, while the latter denotes the idea that an individual is being proactive and is actively in control of his/her learning.

T.I.P. #2
WHY HANDOUTS ARE HANDY!

THEORY: Handouts are invaluable aids not only in helping clients and therapists, but virtually anyone (e.g., those attending a psycho-educational training group session, such as a workplace wellness seminar). Handouts serve as powerful reinforcements and reminders of learning during the session, and help crystallize important therapeutic concepts. Handouts educate in a concise manner. One does not need to sift through an entire book to gain important knowledge to apply to one's life. Handouts are the epitome of practicality—they are targeted to highlight major points in a timely and clear manner.

IMPLEMENTATION: My clients love to get handouts! I knew handouts were a good idea when I witnessed my clients toting them back and forth, circling items, or making notes in the text. I advise that handouts be given out frequently. This workbook provides handouts on a number of topics, or at the very least serves as a basis for clinicians to develop their own handouts. Some handouts simply offer a concise overview of important therapeutic concepts, whereas others require more active participation on the part of the client, entailing responses to questions. The latter are more process-oriented worksheets designed to help the individual tailor the learning to personal thoughts and feelings. These two types of handouts—informational and participatory—work well together to provide opportunities for skill building.

PROCESSING: Handouts help individuals discover for themselves truths that might not be readily apparent. In addition, handouts limit the defensiveness of a client who can use this method of learning to discover for himself/herself faulty habits of thinking and behavior. When used as a vehicle for developing insight, handouts can be powerful aids! Handouts are great reminders that clients often keep on the family refrigerator, mirror, or glove compartment, or even in their wallets or purses. They are light and portable, and can provide structure, guidance, and assistance on an "as needed" basis.

COMMUNICATION QUOTES

"The greatest compliment that was ever paid me was when someone asked me what I thought, and attended to my answer."

—Henry David Thoreau

* * *

"The most important thing in communication is to hear what isn't being said."

—Peter F. Drucker

* * *

"To effectively communicate, we must realize that we are all different in the way we perceive the world and use this understanding as a guide to our communication with others."

—Anthony Robbins

* * *

"You cannot shake hands with a clenched fist."

—Indira Ghandhi

* * *

"Kind words can be short and easy to speak but their echoes are truly endless."

—Mother Theresa

Interpersonal Communication Basics

T.I.P.s #3 & #4
COMMUNICATION SKILLS

THEORY: Despite the fact that communication underlies almost everything we do, it is not uncommon for people to be sorely lacking in knowledge of communication basics. This results in miscommunication, and the fallout results in unhealthy relationships. All too often there is a lack of commonly understood guidelines of what is indeed effective communication. These handouts provide easy to understand differentiation between the three major types of communication. Without this basic knowledge, individuals have limited insight about how they really come across to others, and also lack the tools to make their communication more effective.

T.I.P. #3 Handout: The Three Types of Communication

T.I.P. #4 Handout: Effective Versus Ineffective Communication

IMPLEMENTATION: These two handouts can be used independently or together when dealing with individuals, couples, or groups. They have proven to be enlightening for my clients who have been confused about how their communication can go awry. In addition, these handouts shed insight into how to change unhealthy patterns into more assertive patterns. This is a particularly powerful tool in marriage counseling, as this provides an objective way for individuals to assess their communication styles. It never fails to amaze me that the most non-assertive or aggressive, defensive spouses will correctly identify themselves as either non-assertive or aggressive when seeing it on paper, despite the fact that before presentation of the handout, they deny having major communication problems. It becomes a "no brainer!" These handouts not only demonstrate what is maladaptive but also give clear ideas of healthier messages to replace unhealthy ones.

PROCESSING: With the help of these practical handouts, clients can identify their patterns and identify their style of communication. Often these patterns are learned early on and often are a product of socialization (e.g., women are more rewarded in some societies for being non-assertive, men for being more aggressive). Once the basics of communication are understood, one can readily differentiate between the aggressive "you" versus the assertive "I" focus. In no time, healthier patterns are put into practice, and the results are almost immediate!

THE THREE TYPES OF COMMUNICATION

Non-Assertive Behavior	Assertive Behavior	Aggressive Behavior
Characteristics	***Characteristics***	***Characteristics***
Ignores, does not express own rights, needs, desires	"I" statements Expresses and asserts own rights, needs, desires	"You" statements Expresses own rights at expense of others
Permits others to infringe on his/her rights	Stands up for legitimate rights in a way that rights of others are not violated	Inappropriate outburst or hostile overreaction, intent to humiliate or to "get even," puts others down
Indirect, inhibited	Emotionally honest, direct, expressive	Emotionally honest, direct, expressive at other's expense
Self-denying	Self-enhancing	Self-enhancing
Feelings That Result	***Feelings That Result***	***Feelings That Result***
Hurt, anxious, disappointed in self at the time and possibly angry later	Confident, self-respecting, feels good about self at the time and later	Angry, then righteous, superior, resentful, possibly guilty later
Effects	***Effects***	***Effects***
Avoids unpleasant and risky situations, avoids conflict, feels "used," accumulates anger, feels non-valued	Feels good, valued by self and others, feels better about self, improves self-confidence, needs are met, relationships are freer and more honest	Saving up anger, resentment justifies a blow-up or an emotional outburst, "getting even"

Judith A. Belmont, M.S. (2006) • *86 T.I.P.S. for the Therapeutic Toolbox* • www.worksiteinsights.com •

EFFECTIVE VERSUS INEFFECTIVE COMMUNICATION

Effective Communication	Ineffective Communication

"I" Statements
Excuse me, I would like to finish my statement.

"You" Statements
You're interrupting me again!

Objective/Descriptive Statements
You don't seem to be grasping my point.

Inferential Statements
You're not listening to me!

Non-Evaluative Statements
I have the impression that you view women to be not as capable as men.

Evaluative/Judgmental Statements
You sound like a male chauvinist!

Specific Statements
I'm concerned that you've been late to work the last few days.

Over-Catastrophizing Statements
You're always coming in late to work!

Taking Responsibility
I think we're going off the issue.

Blaming/Giving "Shoulds"
You're taking me off the issue!

Tactful Statements
I don't agree with that.

Tactless Statements
That was a stupid thing to say!

Asking/Requesting
I got the coffee last meeting, so I'd prefer someone else got it today.

Demanding
I got the coffee last time. Someone else should get it today!

Honest Statements
I won't be able to make it at that time for the meeting, so I'd like to see if we could agree on another time.

Dishonest Statement
I wouldn't be able to make it at that time for the meeting, but it really doesn't matter to me, as long as it's convenient for everyone else.

Praising Specifically
You were very considerate to help me on the problem I was having with the proposal.

Praising Generally
You're a considerate person.

Showing Empathy
I can understand why you're concerned about that, but I don't personally feel that will cause a problem.

Minimizing/Devaluing
Don't worry! It's not worth it!

23

Communication Enhancers	Communication Stoppers
I don't see it that way.	That's ridiculous!
I don't think that it will work.	That will never work!
I don't feel you have grasped my point.	You're not listening to me!
I don't feel like it's practical.	It's just not practical.
I'd be surprised if that happened.	It's impossible.
There are times I feel as though you aren't there when I need you.	You're never available!
That happens quite often.	That always happens!
It would be difficult to do that.	There's no way that can be done!
I get angry when you say that.	You make me so mad!
I would appreciate it if you didn't do that.	You shouldn't do that.
That sounds unrealistic to me.	Let's go back to reality.
I don't agree with you.	That's wrong!

T.I.P. #5
COMMUNICATION MADE EVEN SIMPLER . . . FOR KIDS OF ALL AGES

THEORY: The importance of communication cannot be overstated. So much that goes awry in human relationships is a byproduct of unhealthy and problematic communication. Teaching communication skills in a simple way that even children can understand can set up lifelong patterns of healthy relationships and positive "self-talk." Too often the aggressive or non-assertive messages toward others also reverberate in our own inner self-evaluations, leading to extreme perfectionism and low self-esteem.

T.I.P. #5 Handout: Communication Skills Made Easy!

IMPLEMENTATION: This handout can be used even with young children, whether in mental health settings or in a classroom environment. This is especially easy for the less verbal individual or younger client to comprehend and can be used as a supplement to the more informative, detailed T.I.P.s #3 and #4.

PROCESSING: Even the very young client can grasp the lessons of the owl, lion, and turtle. In very simple terms, clients can identify characteristics of healthy and unhealthy communication. This handout can serve as a springboard for discussion of how to understand and deal with various encounters, whether with bullies or with one's closest friends.

COMMUNICATION SKILLS MADE EASY!

Assertive

Wise Communicator

"I" Statements: "I think . . . " "I feel . . . " "It is important to me. . . ."

Respects self and others

"I'm O.K., you're O.K."

Non-Assertive

Passive

"You're O.K., I stink!"

"I need your approval."

"I can't stand conflict."

"Don't make waves."

Indirect, beats around the bush

Aggressive

"I'm O.K., but not too sure about you!"

"Because I said so!"

"I've kept things in too long so no wonder why I explode!"

Might makes right!

"You" statements!

"You make me so mad!"

Judith A. Belmont, M.S. (2006) • *86 T.I.P.S. for the Therapeutic Toolbox* • www.worksiteinsights.com • All rights reserved.

T.I.P.s #6 & #7
BEHIND THE SCENES OF NON-ASSERTIVENESS AND AGGRESSIVENESS

THEORY: After identifying the three types of communication, insight into the reasons, payoffs, and effects of non-assertive and aggressive behavior are invaluable in understanding what goes on "behind the scenes." These handouts give insight into the "whys" behind maladaptive communication styles.

T.I.P. #6 Handout: Non-Assertive Behavior—Reasons and Payoffs

T.I.P. #7 Handout: Aggressive Behavior—Reasons and Payoffs

IMPLEMENTATION: After the introduction to the three communication types, offer a more in-depth view of what makes such individuals tick. Ask clients if they can identify with any of these characteristics in themselves or others. These handouts are particularly helpful in offering a client a "behind the scenes" view of why one would act either non-assertively or aggressively. I warn my clients that non-assertive behavior leads to eventual aggressiveness, as anger, tension, and stress build inside to a boiling point.

PROCESSING: I point out to clients that the payoffs of non-assertive and aggressive behavior are limited and work only for the short term. In the long run, dysfunctional ways of communication lead to alienation, isolation, conflict, and distress. In viewing these objective handouts, clients can readily see why non-assertive and aggressive behaviors have limited potential and can lead to much disappointment and heartache.

NON-ASSERTIVE BEHAVIOR—REASONS AND PAYOFFS

REASONS:

1. *Mistaking Assertion for Aggression:* Assertive behavior mislabeled, often in women, as "masculine" or "aggressive"; consequent confusion over limits for assertive behavior.

2. *Irrational Thought Blocks:* Overcatastrophized, distorted situations leading to anxiety about negative consequences (e.g., fear of losing social approval or of sounding stupid) and interpreting this as being proof of self being a stupid person (generalizing from a specific).

3. *Mistaking Non-Assertiveness for Politeness:* "Shoulds" we have been taught (e.g., "Be agreeable," "Don't make waves," "You mustn't get angry," "Accommodate").

4. *Fear of Change or Disapproval:* Fear of the unknown, including fear of disapproval, making one feel "stuck" in old patterns. Self-doubt replaces action.

5. *Mistaking Non-Assertiveness for Being Helpful:* Unhealthy need to rescue another; taking responsibility for others in not wanting to hurt their feelings or make them upset.

6. *Lack of Assertive Skills:* Individual is used to old behavior pattern and simply does not know how to act otherwise.

PAYOFFS:

Appeases others

Avoids conflict—doesn't "make waves" or "cause a scene"

No risks involved—you're "safe," "secure"

Avoids chance of failure—quiet discomfort preferable to defeat

Substitutes complaining for doing—easier to blame and moan than confront oneself and take the risk of change

Avoids new and anxiety-provoking situations

Is easier in the short run (although more difficult in the long run)

EMOTIONAL TOLL:

Anxiety	Less victimization of control/loss of control
Dependency	Sense of entrapment and victimization
Low self-esteem	Depression
Tension	Sense of inferiority
Anger	Psychosomatic problems
Resentment	

28

Judith A. Belmont, M.S. (2006) • *86 T.I.P.S. for the Therapeutic Toolbox* • www.worksiteinsights.com • All rights reserved.

AGGRESSIVE BEHAVIOR—REASONS AND PAYOFFS

REASONS:

1. *Prior Nonassertion:* Rights violated one too many times and built-up hurt, anger, and tension explodes inappropriately after indirectly taken out on another person.

2. *Need for Control and Dominance:* "Attack before you are attacked"; show strength above all; being in control means to control others.

3. *Overreaction Due to Past Emotional Experience:* Unresolved emotions inappropriately played out in present situations.

4. *Mistaken View of Aggression as Most Desirable:* Belief that aggression is the only way to be effective, get needs met, and be respected.

5. *Skills Deficit:* Individual does not know how to act otherwise and change old habits; inability to handle frustration.

PAYOFFS:

Let off steam

Gain sense of power and control

Can feel superior, mighty

Get immediate needs met

Feel sense of effectiveness

Refuse to be taken advantage of

Seem "strong," hide weakness and vulnerability

Avoid risk of revealing oneself, especially one's human and sensitive side

Can blame others for misfortune while feeling self-righteousness

EMOTIONAL TOLL:

Sense of isolation	Defensiveness
Loneliness	Need to be "on guard"
Alienation	Inability to be human, real
Guilt	Lack of acceptance for self and others

T.I.P. #8
ROADBLOCKS TO COMMUNICATION

THEORY: This handout/worksheet provides another opportunity for clients to receive hands-on practical tips on the topics of communication roadblocks and provides a vehicle to identify more appropriate responses. Awareness of what constitutes roadblocks is a major step toward change.

T.I.P. #8 Handout/Worksheet: Roadblocks to Communication

IMPLEMENTATION: This handout/worksheet can be used as reinforcement for the handouts in T.I.P.s #6 and #7. I usually do not distribute this handout/worksheet at the same time as the others, as I am concerned about stimulus overload. Rather, I use this one a few weeks later as a refresher to both individual and group clients. Ask clients if they identify any of these "roadblocks" in themselves or in others. Brainstorm how they can change the toxic phrases to healthy phrases. You might ask your client to fill in the activity at the bottom of the page and process the answers together.

PROCESSING: Clients find this user-friendly handout/worksheet to be very relevant, as it offers common real-life examples to which many can relate. This can serve as a springboard for discussion on how to handle roadblocks others erect, and can help clients identify the roadblocks they themselves construct.

ROADBLOCKS TO COMMUNICATION

Evaluative—"You should . . ."; "You're wrong . . ."; "You should know that . . ."

Unsolicited Advice—"It would be best for you to . . ."; "Why don't you . . ."

Diagnosing—"You're getting defensive!"

Prying—Puts other on the spot and is intrusive

Commanding—"You had better . . ."; "You have to . . ."

Lecturing—"Don't you realize . . ."

Devaluation Response—"It's not so bad . . ."

Topping—"That's nothing compared to . . ."

Condescending—"I figured you'd do that!"; "I should've expected that from you!"

All or Nothing—"You always do that! Yes you do!"; "You're never . . ."

ACTIVITY: Can you find two types of responses that you have either given or received? Write in the lines below the type of response and the actual statement. Then rewrite the statement in a more effective way.

_____ Type of Response:

Response: _____

Alternative: _____

Take one of the top types of responses and write a statement of what you have actually said to another.

_____ Type of Response:

Response: _____

Alternative: _____

T.I.P. #9
TRANSFORMING "YOU" MESSAGES INTO "I" MESSAGES

THEORY: This worksheet transforms "what" into "how" as the client discovers practical strategies to turn aggressive statements into assertive statements. This worksheet gives hands-on practice to turn around negative messages. It is great for children as well as for adults.

T.I.P. #9 Worksheet: Turn "You" Messages into "I" Messages

IMPLEMENTATION: After clients have been introduced to the concept of the three major types of communication, this worksheet can help differentiate ineffective "you" messages from the more healthy "I" messages. You can ask the client to write responses for a self-help assignment or process responses verbally. This worksheet can be used in either an individual or group setting. Once they have written answers to the items listed, have clients write their own messages that they would like to transform in their own lives.

PROCESSING: This very simple worksheet can go far in giving the individual a sense of empowerment in understanding the delineation between the three types of communication behavior. Explore how transforming these messages can free them from unhealthy habits of communication. Also apply these "I" and "You" statements to "self-talk," as one learns to defeat one's "inner bully." In breaking down dysfunctional habits of thinking, clients can replace irrational thought patterns with more positive thinking habits.

TURN "YOU" MESSAGES INTO "I" MESSAGES

❖ *Why are you being so nosy? It's none of your business!*

I Message:

_____

❖ *You have no right to say that to me!*

I Message:

_____

❖ *You make me so mad!*

I Message:

_____

❖ *You never listen to me!*

I Message:

_____

❖ *Can't you see I am busy now?*

I Message:

_____

❖ *You shouldn't feel that way! You are too sensitive!*

I Message:

_____

Judith A. Belmont, M.S. (2006) • *86 T.I.P.S. for the Therapeutic Toolbox* • www.worksiteinsights.com • All rights reserved.

T.I.P. #10
CHECKLIST FOR ASSERTIVE BEHAVIOR

THEORY: When performing role-plays either in a private or group session, it is helpful to have a checklist to make sure guidelines of assertiveness are being followed. Think of it like an inspection on your car. The car will not "pass" unless certain items are checked off. This checklist offers a user-friendly guide to how to act assertively.

T.I.P. #10 Role-Play and Handout: Checklist for Assertive Behavior

IMPLEMENTATION: Using this handout, ask the client to pick a situation from real life that poses an assertive issue. Go through the checklist before the role-play where you play the person from real life in order to prepare for the interaction, and go over it again after the fact to see if the objectives on the checklist were indeed followed. This provides a step-by-step outline for evaluating the effectiveness of communication in an interpersonal situation.

PROCESSING: This handout provides clear, concise limits for asserting oneself without lapsing into non-assertive or aggressive behavior. Referring to this handout when the "going gets tough" proves to be a very helpful aid for clients hoping to improve their interpersonal skills and composure.

CHECKLIST FOR ASSERTIVE BEHAVIOR

1. Clarify your goal in specific terms.

2. Decide on major points you want to say.

3. Clarify thoughts and feelings.

   • Am I holding on to irrational thoughts?

   • Am I holding on to "should" messages for myself?

   • Am I imposing "should" messages onto the other person?

4. Anticipate positive and negative responses.

   • What's the worst thing that could possibly happen?

   • What's the best thing that could possibly happen?

5. Identify personal rights and corresponding responsibilities.

6. Decide on the proper timing.

7. Weigh the benefits versus risks of being assertive.

8. Relax.

9. Rehearse. Practice an encounter with another person, before a mirror, or in your imagination.

AND REMEMBER! . . .

Use "I" statements.

Don't over-explain or over-apologize.

Don't get sidetracked.

Keep your goal in mind.

Focus on the behavior, not the person.

Be descriptive, not evaluative.

Don't personalize or over-catastrophize.

Another's aggression does not justify counter-aggression.

Don't let someone else set the tone for your own behavior.

Be conscious of expressing sincere praise and positive feedback.

T.I.P. #11
ASSERTIVE AND AGGRESSIVE HUMOR: MAYBE IT'S NOT SO FUNNY!

THEORY: All too often humor is anything but playful and joining, but is rather designed to demean others, or even oneself! After introduction of the concept of the three types of communication earlier in this chapter, focusing on humor that is clean and assertive can help others understand the difference between healthy and cutting humor. Think of how often someone gets offended by another's actions and the person will retort, "just kidding!"

T.I.P. #11 Handout/Worksheet: Assertive Versus Aggressive Humor— Maybe It's Not So Funny!

IMPLEMENTATION: Review with your client the two lists on Assertive and Aggressive Humor, encouraging them to fill in the blanks with their own examples. Spaces at the bottom of the handout are there for clients to generate their own messages, perhaps from those that they have experienced firsthand. Caution that this aggressive style can lead to self-directed aggression, where one also becomes prone to self-disparaging sarcastic humor.

PROCESSING: This is particularly helpful for clients who are "funny" at others' expense and whose mode of communication is sarcasm. This will help people break through the façade of sarcasm to realize that sarcasm is merely disguised aggression. Whether clients are perpetrators or victims of this type of communication, this handout can serve to enlighten and help the change process.

ASSERTIVE VERSUS AGGRESSIVE HUMOR— MAYBE IT'S NOT SO FUNNY!

Assertive humor	Aggressive humor
Builds confidence	Is critical
Accepting	Judgmental
Fun with others	Fun at expense of others
Encourages trust	Breeds anxiety and distrust
Makes closer connections	Alienates others
Supports equality	Gets "one up" on the other
Supportive	Abusive
Shows caring	Shows contempt
Warm	Sarcastic

Below fill in your own adjectives or examples:

_____   _____

_____   _____

_____   _____

_____   _____

T.I.P.s #12 & #13
THE ART OF LISTENING

THEORY: Hearing is not the same thing as listening! People are often so focused on what they say that they are not paying attention to how they listen. They "hear" but often do not "listen." Hearing is taking in audible sounds. Listening requires more activity to integrate messages that are both non-verbal and verbal, as one deciphers actively the message being expressed both verbally and emotionally. Just think of how many altercations and misunderstandings people could avoid by using good listening skills. In "active listening," one hears not what one wants, but understands more what message is being conveyed. The following are excellent handouts for teaching basic life skills—hands-on skills for communicating more effectively through not only what one says but how one listens.

T.I.P. #12 Handout: Tips for Effective Listening

T.I.P. #13 Handout: Active Listening Techniques

IMPLEMENTATION: When using these handouts, ask clients to pick a real-life difficult situation. How can they use these tips to handle the communication in a way that is successful? Brainstorm the difference of how they could have dealt with a problematic situation using active listening. You might want to role-play a situation and show them what it looks like if someone does not use active listening, and then improve upon it to provide a hands-on positive experience. Then you can switch positions so that the client can play the other part. If you are working with a couple having communication problems, these handouts will be ideal resources for improving their ability to listen, and I very often use them to help couples learn to communicate better. I also sometimes use these as a springboard to role-play, having them communicate with one another and then showing each of them how they came across by playing the spouse while they observe.

PROCESS: Encourage clients to use these handouts as guides to ensure they are using good listening skills in their communication. If an interaction goes awry, this is a good way to have them take responsibility for their contribution to the communication and feel empowered that they can change by altering their approach and their attitude. This lesson in active listening, using these sheets as a springboard for role-play, has been invaluable in showing couples how they communicate and how they can change what is not working.

TIPS FOR EFFECTIVE LISTENING

❖ LISTEN FOR THE MESSAGE BEHIND THE WORDS—Hear the other person's feelings, concerns, questions, joys, and fears.

❖ SHOW THAT YOU CARE—Focus on the other person, not yourself; show concern through body language and attentiveness.

❖ SHOW THAT YOU BELIEVE IN THE OTHER PERSON'S ABILITY TO SOLVE HIS/HER OWN PROBLEMS—Suspend your judgments, evaluations, opinions, beliefs, theories, and solutions.

❖ KEEP QUESTIONS TO AN ABSOLUTE MINIMUM—Use only to clarify so you can hear the other person better; keep questions open-ended; do not demand reasons or justifications.

❖ HELP THE PERSON FOCUS ON PARTICULAR PROBLEM AREAS—Summarize and clarify.

❖ STOP WHEN HE/SHE WANTS TO STOP—You might have already helped enough; he/she might not want to continue now.

ACTIVE LISTENING TECHNIQUES

Statements That Help the Other Person Talk

STATEMENT	PURPOSE	SKILLS
ENCOURAGING	To convey interest. To encourage the other person to keep talking.	Don't judge. Use neutral words. Use varying voice intonations.
CLARIFYING	To help you clarify what is said.	Ask questions. Restate wrong interpretation to force speaker to explain further.
RESTATING	To show you are listening and understanding what is being said. To check your meaning and interpretation.	Restate basic ideas, facts.
REFLECTING	To show that you understand how the person feels. To help the person evaluate his/her own feelings after hearing them expressed by someone else.	Reflect the speaker's basic feelings.
SUMMARIZING	To review progress. To pull together important ideas including feelings. To establish a basis for further discussion.	Restate the major ideas expressed.
VALIDATING	To acknowledge the worthiness of the other person.	Acknowledge the value of the other person's issues and feelings. Show appreciation for the other person's efforts and actions.

40

ANGER QUOTES

"Holding on to anger is like grasping a hot coal with the intent of throwing it at someone else; you are the one who gets burned."

—Buddha

* * *

"Anyone can become angry. That is easy. But to be angry with the right person, to the right degree, at the right time, for the right purpose and in the right way . . . that is not easy."

—Aristotle

* * *

"Anger is only one letter short of danger."

—Unknown

* * *

"Nothing gives one person so much advantage over another as to remain always cool and unruffled under all circumstances."

—Thomas Jefferson

* * *

"For every minute you are angry you lose sixty seconds of happiness."

—Ralph Waldo Emerson

Taking the Angst out of Anger

T.I.P. #14
BULLY BUSTING: COVERING THE BUTTONS OF VULNERABILITY

THEORY: Our "buttons" are often too exposed, and we let others push them. I explain to clients that "no one can make you upset—you allow them to." Too often, we leave ourselves at the mercy of others. This worksheet helps one feel more empowered by knowing what "buttons" need to be covered!

T.I.P. #14 Worksheet: Bully Buttons!

IMPLEMENTATION: Ask your client to complete this worksheet in either a written or verbal manner. You might have the client take it home for a self-help assignment or work on it together in the office. This can be used with children as well as adults, as the concept is straightforward and the handout is presented in simple terms.

PROCESSING: Brainstorm with the client how he/she can "cover" those buttons. Discuss situations where the client feels a lack of control, and focus on what the client needs to do to take more control over his/her own reactions. The concept that no one can make you feel a certain way is not a new one but is very difficult for many in their everyday patterns of thinking to keep in mind.

BULLY BUTTONS!

No one can make us angry; we are in charge of our anger! People do not have to push your buttons! Do not make them so accessible! Ideally, they are only yours to push!

DIRECTIONS: Write below the "buttons" that we allow others to push that cause us emotional distress. Then write how you can change your usual response.

Buttons of Vulnerability

EXAMPLE: *I am so angry when my mother makes a comment about my weight.*

Changed Response: _____

_____

MY EXAMPLE: _____

Changed Response: _____

_____

MY EXAMPLE: _____

Changed Response: _____

_____

MY EXAMPLE: _____

Changed Response: _____

_____

T.I.P. #15
TURNING COMPLAINTS INTO GOALS

THEORY: In dealing with the treatment-resistant client, negativity is a common thread. This therapeutic strategy and worksheet help the practitioner transform the complaint and negativity into goal setting. Goal setting promotes a positive framework for growth to occur.

T.I.P. #15 Worksheet: Turning Complaints into Goals

IMPLEMENTATION: In the case of a depressive or negativistic client, use a negative statement and brainstorm how to make these negative ideas into goals. These "subliminal" messages you offer clients help to create a more positive outlook. You might let clients in on what you are doing and go over some of their statements together, writing them down and figuring out together how you can transform them into goals. Or this might be more of a hypnotic and suggestive technique that you can use to reframe negative messages into positive ones. If you discuss this concept openly with the client, the following worksheet can provide some structure to the lesson of "Turning Complaints into Goals."

PROCESSING: Observe how the client responds when a more positive spin is put on his/her negativity. This strategy puts responsibility for change on the client, who now is encouraged to take responsibility for "bad luck." This is not meant to be in response to major life catastrophes but rather to be used when negativity and irrational thinking rule supreme.

TURNING COMPLAINTS INTO GOALS

Complaint   **Goal**

I don't like coming to group! _____

Nothing turns out for me! _____

I hate going to school! _____

I can't stand my job! _____

My life is a mess! _____

I have too much to do in too little time! _____

Life is just not fair! _____

My co-workers are not nice to me! _____

I just don't have enough money! _____

I have hardly any friends! _____

Turning Complaints   ### Into Treatment Goals

> I just have rotten luck!

> Sounds like you're motivated to work harder to increase your odds!

T.I.P. #16
ANGER DIARY

THEORY: For many clients, controlling anger is an enormous challenge. When things go well and a person feels satisfied, it is easier to act in socially acceptable ways. Once anger mounts, however, and the controls are not in place to manage the anger, troubled relationships become more troubled, and ineffective coping mechanisms become more pronounced. This anger diary worksheet is applicable to all populations across the board. This self-help assignment also can be used in Dialectical Behavior Therapy, where anger management helps regulate emotions for high risk clients.

T.I.P. #16 Worksheet: Anger Diary

IMPLEMENTATION: In individual or group sessions, have participants fill in the following worksheet. In either individual or group format, ideas can generate a great amount of insight and sharing. Recognizing how one reacts to anger is the first step to controlling it.

PROCESSING: After this self-reflective exercise, individuals can benefit from sharing their thoughts and ideas. Brainstorm how they might remember their ideas in times of emotional turmoil. Suggest that individuals keep their "Self-Help" notebook/folder and refer to this not only when angry (since by then it might be too late!) but at other times when they are feeling less stressed and angry. This way, in times of anger, new habits already will be well on their way to being established.

ANGER DIARY

Identify my "Anger Trigger": _____

Describe how it feels: _____

Describe my rational self-talk: _____

Describe my irrational self-talk: _____

How did I handle it? _____

Alternative ways to handle it? _____

Check off ideas that "fit me" for managing this anger:

_____ Count to ten before responding   _____ Write a letter

_____ Practice forgiveness   _____ Write feelings in a journal

_____ Write in a journal   _____ Confront the person assertively

_____ Use "I" statements   _____ Draw what you are feeling

_____ Confront the person assertively   _____ Talk it out with a friend

_____ What can you learn from your anger?   _____ Exercise, discharge energy

_____ Identify goals of other's misbehavior   _____ Role-play ways to handle anger

_____ Identify the goals of my misbehavior   _____ Remove yourself from the situation

_____ Identify self-imposed "shoulds"   _____ Express self before a mirror

_____ Identify "shoulds" for others   _____ Use relaxation techniques

_____ Forgive others for being unhealthy   _____ Forgive yourself for being unhealthy

Pick two items that you checked off and elaborate how you can do this below. Or choose two of your own methods for dealing with the anger: _____

_____

_____

_____

T.I.P. #17
S.T.A.R. T.I.P.S. FOR ANGER MANAGEMENT

THEORY: In the midst of anger and emotional upset, those clients having trouble controlling anger can benefit from some practical handouts and strategies to diffuse their anger. You might consider this handout a "cookbook" recipe of how to deal with anger. It offers skills and structure at a time when self-control level is low. This S.T.A.R. T.I.P.S. handout offers help for clients to deal with and handle their negative emotions in a way that is constructive.

T.I.P. #17 Handout: S.T.A.R. T.I.P.S. for Controlling and Expressing Anger

IMPLEMENTATION: When a client expresses anger and rage and admits having difficulty coping, offer this handout. These ideas can guide a client when he/she is in the midst of overwhelming emotion. Ask the client to describe a problematic situation and explain how that triggered an angry reaction. Suggest that having this handout handy can help avert further behavioral problems.

PROCESS: Through this handout, clients can appreciate the universality of out-of-control thinking and anxiety related issues in social situations, and can be encouraged to realize that they are not the "only one." The hands-on T.I.P.S. serve to counteract irrational thinking. Clients can use these tips to identify irrational beliefs and dispute them in life situations that pose predicaments for them.

S.T.A.R. T.I.P.S. FOR CONTROLLING AND EXPRESSING ANGER

Stop.

"I'm not going to allow myself to let someone 'push my buttons'."

Think about what will happen if you lose control.

"If I lose control. . . ."

Ask yourself why you're really angry.

"The real reason I'm angry is. . . ."

Reduce anger.

"I will take some deep breaths. I will walk away. I need to cool down. I'm going to. . . ."

Tell the person how you feel.

"I feel very lonely and sad. . . ."

Identify the specific event that made you feel that way.

"I'm upset because I felt angry when you did . . . because . . ."

Process why this triggered anger in you.

"I think when you yell, I feel like I am a child again and am being punished."

Success! Reward yourself.

"I did a good job! I could control my emotions and take responsibility for them."

T.I.P. #18
A.C.T. N.O.W.!

THEORY: Acronyms can make ideas easier to remember. This handout, "A.C.T. N.O.W.! Control That Temper!" gives a short, simple "recipe" for controlling anger. It encourages the client to "ACT NOW!" rather than wait for things to be better in the future. A.C.T. N.O.W. calls clients to take change NOW and use steps they learned in the therapeutic process to control and manage their anger. This exercise is very helpful in individual and group therapy and can aid the Dialectical Behavior Therapy group when addressing emotional modulation skills.

T.I.P. #18 Handout: A.C.T. N.O.W.! Control That Temper!

IMPLEMENTATION: Using this handout as a guide, discuss with clients how to use these concepts in their own lives. Discussions of steps they need to take to incorporate these principles are vital to filling in the "ingredients" to the recipe.

PROCESSING: Ask clients how this handout can help them in times of emotional turmoil. Brainstorm how they can keep these concepts in the forefront of their mind, even to the point of figuring where they will keep the handout to have it on hand. Do most problems happen at work? At home? Help them prepare so they won't be caught off guard.

ACT NOW! CONTROL THAT TEMPER!

Alter that thinking!

1. No one makes you angry except yourself!
2. Don't let your irrational thoughts take over; control them!
3. It's okay to be angry, but not to be aggressive! One is a behavior; one is an emotion.
4. Change yourself, not the other person!
5. Forgive the other person for the way he/she is.

Change the emotions!

1. Replacing your irrational thoughts with more rational thoughts will result in healthier emotions.
2. Try to accept others for who they are and develop compassion.
3. Try techniques, like counting to ten, relaxation, deep breathing, or imagery before expressing emotions that are overpowering.

Tone down the behaviors!

1. Use "I" statements instead of "you" statements.
2. Role-play and rehearse how to act more appropriately.
3. Reduce the intensity by using a sense of humor.
4. Talking louder will not make people hear you better.
5. Practice active listening skills.

New habits can be developed!

1. Develop new habits and patterns of responding when upset.
2. Reward yourself for new actions taken and little steps toward success.
3. Have confidence in yourself that this can be achieved.

Overcome the obstacles!

1. See obstacles as another opportunity to learn and grow.
2. Avoiding the situation might be easier in the short run but is more difficult in the long run.
3. Allow yourself to be empowered by being more "in control" without being controlling.

Win–Win!

1. With new habits of thought, emotions, and behavior, it's a win–win situation for everyone involved.
2. All are treated with respect while feelings are shared.
3. Experience growth, forgiveness, and a breaking of shackles that hold you back.

T.I.P. #19
ANGER REDUCING RATIONAL BELIEFS

THEORY: This handout helps clients keep in mind rational thinking habits when irrational anger-producing thoughts get out of control. This handout helps one to self-monitor how much anger can "get to them" and helps them keep things in perspective.

T.I.P. #19 Handout: Anger Reducing Rational Beliefs

IMPLEMENTATION: If a client's anger appears to be out of control and there is evidence of irrational, distorted, out-of-control thinking, use this handout to offer a more rational perspective to the client's angst, which will calm the client down from distorted ways of thinking. Have the client think of his/her last argument or conflict, and ask what items on this handout could have helped to quell the conflict.

PROCESSING: Brainstorm with the client how this handout can help keep arguments and conflicts in perspective. Although these are simple concepts, assure the client that it is easier said than done!

ANGER REDUCING RATIONAL BELIEFS

Anger toward others prevents me from getting what I want.

I wish they would act differently, but it is not healthy to "should" on them!

I wish others would treat me fairly, but they do not *have* to.

I can put up with a negative, hostile person even though I wish he/she would act better.

While it is preferable to be treated kindly, fairly, and considerately, there is no law that says I *must* be.

I can no longer let someone else set the tone for my behavior, as I am responsible for my behavior.

I really *can* stand what I don't like; it just is upsetting.

I need to forgive the other person for not being as healthy as I would have wished.

Will I remember this ten years from now? One year from now? I week from now? If not, it is not worth spending so much energy and emotion on this.

Fill in your own rational beliefs

_____

_____

_____

_____

_____

Judith A. Belmont, M.S. (2006) • *86 T.I.P.S. for the Therapeutic Toolbox* • www.worksiteinsights.com • All rights reserved.

THOUGHTFUL QUOTES

"Nothing is good or bad but thinking makes it so."

—Shakespeare

* * *

"People are not disturbed by things, but by the view they take of them."

—Epictetus

* * *

"If you judge people, you have no time to love them."

—Mother Teresa

* * *

"We are what we think. All that we are arises with our thoughts. With our thoughts we make the world."

—Buddha

* * *

"The happiness of your life depends on the quality of your thoughts."

—Marcus Aurelius

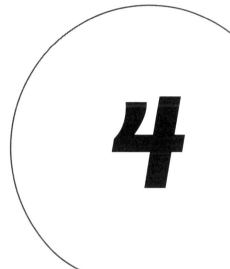

Cognitive Therapy at Work!

T.I.P.s #20–#24
DEFEATING IRRATIONAL THINKING

THEORY: All too often in counseling I observe clients thinking and talking in inflexible, extreme, negative ways that are unhealthy. These practical, educational handouts for clients introduce them to cognitive restructuring principles. These handouts have helped hundreds of clients gain more control and insight into defeating unwanted irrational thoughts and emotions. The following five handouts are among my favorites and have been very successful in making cognitive behavioral concepts clear in a short period of time. Hope-inspiring ideas replace pessimistic and self-defeating ones.

T.I.P. #20 Handout: Albert Ellis' Common Irrational Beliefs

T.I.P. #21 Handout: Rational Versus Irrational Thoughts

T.I.P. #22 Handout: Going to Extremes

T.I.P. #23 Handout: How to Recognize Distorted Beliefs

T.I.P. #24 Handout: Steps for Changing Irrational Beliefs

IMPLEMENTATION: Using the following handouts, ask clients to identify what items they can relate to; handouts can be completed as homework or in session. Use the sheets as a springboard to educate clients on the main ideas of cognitive therapy. On many occasions clients have brought back these handouts and circled for themselves what they are stuck on, even before being prompted to do so. I enjoy supplying various types of handouts, as sometimes one "clicks" more than another, and an array of possible teaching tools gives wider possibilities for educating and enlightening.

PROCESSING: These handouts are particularly helpful for those who experience anxiety, depression, and excess distress, but all types of clients can find them quite helpful and educational. Clients often are amazed that feelings and thoughts are not the same and need to be distinguished from one another. This idea in itself can be enlightening. Invariably, with practice, even the most treatment-resistant client is able to identify patterns of unhealthy thinking.

ALBERT ELLIS' COMMON IRRATIONAL BELIEFS

Irrational Belief	Rational Counterpart
One should be liked and approved of by almost everyone.	No one is liked by everyone. That is unrealistic!
To be worthy and have self-esteem, one must be competent in all respects.	One cannot expect to be perfect in all respects; it's okay to make mistakes!
Some people are just plain bad!	Behaviors are bad; people might be extremely unhealthy.
Things should be the way we want them to be; it's terrible when they aren't.	Things are not always the way we want them to be, but that's not the end of the world. We can still function.
Individuals have little internal control over their personal happiness or misery.	We can exercise a great deal of control over our own happiness or make our misery worse.
If there is some possibility that something can go wrong, it's okay to worry excessively even though you can't change it.	It is good to be proactive if we can "do" something, but excessive worrying won't help.
It is easier to avoid than to face difficulties and problems; hopefully they will just go away.	In the long run, it's better to face difficulties and accept responsibilities; only then can there be resolution and healing.
I really need to be dependent upon someone stronger than myself. My happiness depends on others.	I'm the one who ultimately decides what's best for me. Dependency is more a habit and a state of mind that can be altered with practice.
We're all products of our past history; we can't change anything. I've always been this way!	Certainly past events influence our behavior, but we can learn to modify a great deal of how we think and react if we work at it. People can and do change.
There is a right and perfect way to do everything, and it's catastrophic if we don't find that way.	There is not always an ideal solution. Rather, there are often several somewhat effective approaches to a task.

RATIONAL VERSUS IRRATIONAL THOUGHTS

Irrational Thoughts That Cause Disturbance	Rational Thoughts That Promote Emotional Self-Control
1. How *awful*.	This is disappointing.
2. I can't stand it.	I can put up with what I don't like.
3. I'm stupid	What I *did* was stupid.
4. He stinks!	He's not perfect, either.
5. This *shouldn't* have happened.	This should have happened because it did!
6. I am to be blamed.	I am at fault, but I am not to be blamed.
7. He has no right.	He has every right to follow his own mind, though I wish he wouldn't have exercised that right!
8. I *need* him/her to do that.	I want/desire/prefer him/her to do that, but I don't have to have what I want.
9. Things *always* go wrong.	Sometimes things will go wrong.
10. *Every time* I try, I fail.	Sometimes—even often—I may fail.
11. Things *never* work out.	More often than I would like, things don't work out.
12. This is bigger than life.	This is an important *part* of my life.
13. This *should* be easier.	I wish this were easier, but often things aren't; no pain, no gain. Tough. Too bad!
14. I *should* have done better.	I would have *preferred* to do better, but I did what I could at the time.
15. I am a failure.	I'm a person who sometimes fails.

(Adapted from *RET Resource Book*, 1991, Bernard & Wolfe, Eds.)

GOING TO EXTREMES . . .

1. I can't stand it!
2. It is terrible that things go wrong!
3. He shouldn't be that way!
4. People ought to do what I wish!
5. They should listen to me!
6. I can't change what I think!
7. My emotions can't be controlled!
8. I should be able to control my kids' behavior!
9. I can't forgive them/myself.
10. He makes me nuts!
11. It's awful!
12. He always does that!
13. He is much too sensitive!
14. She never does that!
15. I need him!
16. I should have done that!
17. Things must be different!
18. I should be better!
19. The world ought to be fair!
20. She made me feel that way!
21. It drives me crazy!
22. He ruined my life!
23. Things are hopeless!
24. I hate being criticized!
25. He must love me!
26. My childhood always will affect me!
27. It's terrible to be wrong!
28. I can't control my feelings!
29. I can't help the way I act!
30. I can change him!
31. I'm responsible for her feelings!
32. It's my fault she is like that!
33. He made me do that!
34. She makes me act that way!
35. Strong people don't ask for help!
36. I'd be happy if only . . .
37. I must depend on others!
38. He has to understand!
39. People should be more like me!
40. I can't stand the way others act.

HOW TO RECOGNIZE THINKING THAT IS DISTORTED AND IRRATIONAL

VERY EXTREME—Seeing things in black and white, and blowing things out of proportion

VERY BROAD—Generalizing from a specific; labeling people rather than their behaviors

VERY CATASTROPHIC—Exaggerating how "awful" something is when these thoughts are better reserved for life and death situations or events of serious injury

VERY NEGATIVE—Seeing the glass as half empty not half full and dwelling heavily on the negative

VERY SKEWED—Skewing your perceptions to fit your idiosyncratic "proofs"

VERY UNSCIENTIFIC—Ignoring the facts; preferring to go on "gut" and feeling in a non-constructive way

VERY IDEALISTIC—Denying and having unrealistic expectations that cloud a sense of reality

VERY DEMANDING—Wanting things your way and having expectations that also include being demanding of yourself

VERY JUDGMENTAL—Condemning others for their shortcomings and being unable to forgive

VERY OBSESSED—Getting on a track of thinking and being unable to budge or view things differently; perseverating about something that is out of your control

VERY CONFUSED—Having pictures in your head that do not match the "real world"; feeling that you don't get what you think you are "supposed to" get; having a hard time seeing things without delusion, denial, and negativity

VERY INTOLERANT—Having a need to have things the way they "should be"; finding it difficult to have patience and tolerance for differences that don't fit your needs and expectations

VERY PERFECTIONISTIC—Having a need to be "right" and not make mistakes, as that would mean one is inferior or is a failure; having permeating low self-esteem

"SHOULDING" ON SELF AND OTHERS—Placing expectations of how one "should" be, thereby limiting one's ability to accept self and others without judgment, leading to negativity and tendency to criticize

LABELING AND INTERPRETING—Blowing mistakes out of proportion, leading to labeling self or others as a "failure" or a "bum"

STEPS FOR CHANGING IRRATIONAL BELIEFS

STEP 1   **Recognize the irrational belief.**

Try to find the "inner script" that leads to problematic thinking, and uncover the "musts," "shoulds," "can'ts," and extreme thinking that gets one into trouble!

STEP 2   **Decide whether or not to change.**

Weigh the gains versus the losses involved in changing your behavior in this situation and decide whether the possible gains will be worth the risks involved.

STEP 3   **Formulate a more rational belief (rB) to substitute for the irrational belief (iB). Dispute the automatic, irrational one!**

Use "Ellis' Common Irrational Beliefs" handout for suggestions on some rational alternatives to substitute for certain irrational ideas. Try to reformulate the statement of the rational idea until it fits your style and you believe it.

STEP 4   **Act in light of the new, rational belief.**

Force yourself to act this way even though it feels phony. *Make* opportunities to practice acting in light of your new beliefs. This will, most probably, involve taking some risks. Use assertive communication skills.

STEP 5   **Continue to behave in the new, more rational way.**

Again, force yourself to maintain your new behavior pattern. If you do, you will automatically stop behaving in the old way, and the new way will become part of your "natural" behavior. Habits are not changed overnight. Try to be patient!

(Based on books by Maxie Maultsby and Albert Ellis.)

T.I.P.s #25–#30
COGNITIVE THERAPY AT WORK!

THEORY: The concepts of Cognitive Behavioral Therapy have been so simple yet so profound in enlightening clients to the pitfalls of erroneous thinking. What seems to be common sense is not so obvious when one is mired in negative thought habits and patterns. Along with read-only handouts, worksheets in which clients can fill out their own responses to practice strategies can be quite helpful. The following activities have been indispensable aids to educating and providing insight for clients who have been unaware of how irrational self-talk has robbed them of peace of mind and has led to damaging relationships.

T.I.P. #25 Worksheet: Counterproductive Thinking

T.I.P. #26 Worksheet: Rational Thinking at Work!

T.I.P. #27 Worksheet: My Common Mental Mistakes

T.I.P. #28 Worksheet: Rational Self-Help Form—Dissecting an Irrational Event (ABCDE)

T.I.P. #29 Worksheet: ABCDE Diary (Diary for Identifying, Challenging, and Changing Irrational Beliefs)

T.I.P. #30 Worksheet: Real-Life ABCDEs—Disputing and Decatastrophizing

IMPLEMENTATION: These handouts either summarize types of irrational thinking patterns, with a short activity at the bottom, or are total worksheets on the subject. I ask clients to share an example from their life, and we use the sheets to help dissect the situation. Choose at most a couple of these activities to use at one time for clients' "Self-Help" assignments, to be used as guides to fill out for the next session. If handouts/worksheets are given out gradually there is more time for digestion, incorporation, and reinforcement of the information. Looking at negative self-talk in such an objective, matter-of-fact manner is especially helpful for the well defended client.

PROCESSING: These handouts and worksheets provide a great springboard for discussions about unhealthy thinking patterns. These short self-help exercises encourage active participation and collaboration, so the client assumes increasing responsibility in the therapeutic process of "getting better."

COUNTERPRODUCTIVE THINKING

1. **ALL OR NOTHING THINKING**—You see things in black or white categories. If you make a mistake, you might think that you "failed" and/or are a "failure."

2. **OVERGENERALIZATION**—You think in absolutes, like "always" and "never," and see a single negative event as a never-ending pattern—generalizing from a specific.

3. **MENTAL FILTER**—You pick out a negative single event and dwell on it, like a drop of ink that discolors a whole beaker of water. You do not seek to change your attitude and viewpoint.

4. **MAGNIFY AND CATASTROPHIZE**—You blow things out of proportion. A good rule of thumb is that if you won't remember this a year from now, it is not worth being as upset about.

5. **SHOULD STATEMENTS**—Living in the world of "woulda, coulda, shoulda" becomes tedious and sets one up for a lot misery. Accepting things as they are if you cannot change them is more adaptive, and to work on changing only yourself and things under your control is your only healthy option. Directing "shoulds" toward others only engenders distrust, anger, and friction.

6. **PERSONALIZATION**—You take on more responsibility than is really yours and blame yourself for others' problems and behaviors, or vice versa, seeing yourself as a victim of others. Also, with extreme sensitivity, you take things too personally rather than see others' negative actions toward you as a reflection more of them than you.

7. **PLAYING THE COMPARISON GAME**—Comparing yourself to others and needing to keep up with or outshine others to feel good about yourself; jealousy abounds.

What negative thoughts or patterns create stress in you?

1.

2.

How could you replace those thoughts with more positive, rational thoughts?

1.

2.

Judith A. Belmont, M.S. (2006) • *86 T.I.P.S. for the Therapeutic Toolbox* • www.worksiteinsights.com • All rights reserved.

RATIONAL THINKING AT WORK!

Common Irrational Beliefs	Rational Beliefs
Perfectionism—It's awful to make mistakes.	It's okay to make mistakes.
He/she is more liked than me.	I am not in a race with others.
I have to be as good.	Their success does not diminish mine.
I must be approved of by those I care about.	It would be nice but is not necessary.
I equate performance with self-worth.	I am worthy regardless.
I can't stand these people.	I can put up with what I do not like.
They should be more fair.	It would be nice if they were more fair.
I HATE this job!	I am not happy in this job.
They make me so mad.	No one makes me mad; I have the power.
They are bad.	They might be unhealthy.
I should be further along in my career.	I am going in the right direction.
I feel like a failure.	I'm not happy with my accomplishments.
This is a crappy job.	I don't like this job and need to find another.

ACTIVITY: Fill in your own irrational beliefs pertaining to work and then find a more rational alternative for each:

_____   _____

_____   _____

_____   _____

_____   _____

_____   _____

MY COMMON MENTAL MISTAKES

Judith A. Belmont, M.S. (2006) • *86 T.I.P.S. for the Therapeutic Toolbox* • www.worksiteinsights.com • All rights reserved.

RATIONAL SELF-HELP FORM—
DISSECTING AN IRRATIONAL EVENT (ABCDE)

Activating Event _____

Beliefs _____

Consequence _____

Feelings _____

Behavior _____

Disputing _____

Effect of more rational thinking _____

(Replace with more rational belief)

ABCDE DIARY

(Diary for Identifying, Challenging, and Changing Irrational Beliefs)

A	B	C	D	E
Activating Event	*Belief*	*Consequences*	*Disputing Irrational Belief*	*Effects of Rational Beliefs*

REAL-LIFE ABCDES—DISPUTING AND DECATASTROPHIZING

Strategies for "Thought Catching"

My ABC Diary

	Adversity	Beliefs	Consequences
1.	_____	_____	_____
2.	_____	_____	_____
3.	_____	_____	_____

Questions:

- Where is the evidence that the belief is true?

- What is an alternative way to view the situation?

- What is the worst thing that could happen? Is it likely?

- What is the best thing that could happen? Is it likely?

- What is my plan of attack?

ADVERSITY _____

(The factual aspects of the negative event—who, what, where—that posed a problem. Be specific.)

BELIEFS _____

(The belief and interpretations about the Adversity.)

CONSEQUENCES _____

(How you feel and behave following the Adversity.)

DISPUTATIONS _____

(Self-disputing the irrational, pessimistic, and exaggerated beliefs.)

ENERGIZATIONS _____

(The emotional and behavioral consequences of your Disputation.)

(Adapted from Martin Seligman's "The Optimistic Child," developed from his work in the Penn Prevention Program.)

T.I.P. #31
RATIONAL AND IRRATIONAL THINKING IN MEETINGS

THEORY: Using common examples to illustrate points is usually an effective way of teaching and enlightening. It is not unusual for a client to have difficulty speaking in front of a group, and thus most people can relate to this example of having difficulty speaking up at a meeting. In the handout, irrational thought is replaced with more rational alternatives.

T.I.P. #31 Handout: Rational and Irrational Thinking in Meetings

IMPLEMENTATION: I introduce this handout to clients as an example of putting rational thinking skills into practice. This is a very direct and practical example of how irrational thoughts create irrational emotions and behaviors, while rational thoughts create rational feelings and emotions. I ask clients to identify if there are any messages here that they can relate to. The answer is invariably yes, since I pull this handout out most often in situations of social anxiety and social phobia in which clients are terrified of saying the wrong thing!

PROCESSING: This powerful and self-explanatory handout can really hit home to the individual fraught with social anxieties and offers some comfort that "Wow, other people think this way too!" Just knowing you are not alone does wonders for the psyche, and the fact that there are practical ideas for reframing and replacing negative self-talk makes this an ideal handout for any client, but particularly those with social anxiety.

RATIONAL AND IRRATIONAL THINKING IN MEETINGS

IRRATIONAL THOUGHTS	RATIONAL ALTERNATIVES
• If I disagree, they might not like me.	• I have to separate my idea from me.
• I HATE making mistakes!	• It's human to make mistakes.
• They might think that what I have to say is stupid, which would mean I'm a stupid person.	• I'm generalizing from a specific. Also, I have a right to make a mistake.
• I don't want to "make waves" or "cause a scene."	• That is overcatastrophizing; it is not likely that things will go to that extreme.
• I don't want to take up everybody else's time.	• My time is as important as everyone else's. I have a right to speak my mind.
• Maybe they're RIGHT and I'm WRONG! That would be TERRIBLE and AWFUL!	• Again, that is overcatastrophizing. TERRIBLE is a little strong.
• I must be competent at all times!	• Trying my best is all I can do—I am not perfect.
• I can't stand rejection and failure!	• I can stand disappointment and shortcomings.
• I need everybody to approve of me at all times.	• It would be nice, but impossible. Better to work on liking myself.
• They might get annoyed with me for disagreeing.	• I can't be responsible for their reactions.

IRRATIONAL FEELINGS	RATIONAL FEELINGS
• Depressed, worthless	• Positive, self-accepting
• Anxious	• Calm
• Angry	• Forgiving
• Insecure, lack of confidence	• Confident, secure
• Psychosomatic reactions: Clammy palms, headache, heart thumping	• Physically relaxed and feeling healthy

IRRATIONAL BEHAVIORS	RATIONAL BEHAVIORS
• Remain silent	• Speak up confidently
• Withdraw from people after the meeting	• Be friendly with coworkers after meeting
• Overeat, over-drink	• Deal with any disagreement
• Take anger out on clients, coworkers, family	• Deal positively with coworkers, clients, family
• Feel immobilized and victimized	• Learn from the experience

T.I.P.s #32–#34
QUESTIONNAIRES AND SURVEYS ON SELF-TALK HABITS

THEORY: Because I have found hands-on activities to be so effective at helping clients, I also share with them questionnaires to help them assess the prevalence of irrational thoughts that interfere with their emotional resiliency.

T.I.P. #32 Worksheet: Questionnaire on Self-Talk

T.I.P. #33 Worksheet: Survey on Thought Habits

T.I.P. #34 Worksheet: "You Are Your Own Worst Enemy" Checklist

IMPLEMENTATION: I ask clients to complete these worksheets either in session or in between sessions, and then go over the results with them. Items that display irrational thinking are addressed, as well as reinforcement for the more healthy responses. If they answer honestly, they often are surprised at the amount of irrational ideas they possess that go undetected!

PROCESSING: Self-talk improves with insight, and these questionnaires provide yet another way to help clients identify irrational beliefs and replace them with more rational alternatives to promote positive self-talk. These worksheets are successful in both individual counseling and group counseling (where results can be shared either within smaller sub-groups or within the whole group).

QUESTIONNAIRE ON SELF-TALK

Circle **YES** or **NO**

YES   **NO**   My thoughts and feelings are interchangeable—one and the same.

YES   **NO**   Other people should be more considerate of me.

YES   **NO**   My feelings control my thoughts.

YES   **NO**   I am too sensitive.

YES   **NO**   My family controls me too much.

YES   **NO**   My friends control me too much.

YES   **NO**   I can't get over this negative mood I have.

YES   **NO**   A situation can make me go into a depression or even just a funk.

YES   **NO**   When something goes wrong, there are times I cannot tolerate it.

YES   **NO**   I should be further along in my life by now.

Look at how many "yes" responses there are. Challenge the "no" responses with the concepts below about "cause and effect."

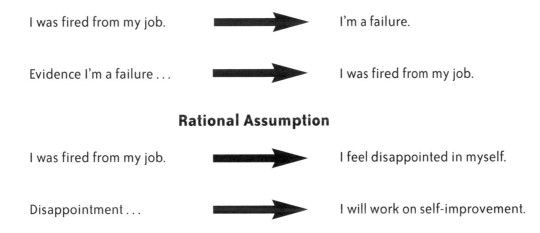

Common Irrational Assumptions About Cause and Effect

I was fired from my job. ➡ I'm a failure.

Evidence I'm a failure . . . ➡ I was fired from my job.

Rational Assumption

I was fired from my job. ➡ I feel disappointed in myself.

Disappointment . . . ➡ I will work on self-improvement.

SURVEY ON THOUGHT HABITS

_____ 1. How many people at work make you upset?

_____ 2. How many people cause you emotional upset?

_____ 3. Count the things in your life that are totally unbearable.

_____ 4. Count the things you are faced with that are awful and terrible.

_____ 5. How many things can you not stand?

_____ 6. Estimate how many times in a week things don't go the way they should.

_____ 7. How many people do you know who are always critical?

_____ 8. In a given month, how many times do you feel that awful events keep happening to you?

_____ 9. Count how many of your family members upset you.

_____ 10. How many times in a week do people disappoint you?

_____ 11. How many times in a week do you disappoint yourself?

_____ 12. Estimate the number of times you have failed in your life.

_____ 13. I shouldn't have to work so hard at what is natural for others.

_____ 14. Estimate how many times in a given week you cannot control your feelings.

_____ 15. How many times in a given week do you feel hopeless?

_____ 16. How many times on average weekly do you think "I can't take this!"?

Add all the numbers: _____

0–3   Extremely healthy thought habits

4–7   Moderately distressing thought habits

8–12   Severely disturbing and irrational thought habits

13 +   Danger zone! Many unhealthy thought habits pave the way for depression, anxiety, and stress-related health problems.

Judith A. Belmont, M.S. (2006) • *86 T.I.P.S. for the Therapeutic Toolbox* • www.worksiteinsights.com • All rights reserved.

"YOU ARE YOUR OWN WORST ENEMY" CHECKLIST

Check the box if you have a tendency to do this self-downing:

☐   If I make a mistake, I feel like I failed.

☐   If things don't go well, I feel hopeless.

☐   If I get rejected by people, I feel like a loser.

☐   When people are more accomplished than me, I feel inadequate.

☐   If someone rejects me, I feel unlikable.

☐   If I did something foolish, I feel like a fool.

☐   When I go off of my diet, I feel like I'm out of control.

☐   If I am wrong, I need to prove why I am right.

☐   I can't stand being wrong, since that would reflect badly on me as a person.

☐   If someone else is right, that means he/she is better than me.

☐   I like to get "the last word" so that no one puts anything over me.

☐   I do not like where I am in my life; I feel like I failed.

For any item checked, rephrase the sentence into a less punitive and more rational alternative:

_____

_____

_____

_____

_____

T.I.P. #35
FACT VERSUS FICTION ACTIVITY

THEORY: All too often we treat interpretations as if they were facts. When supplying ourselves with negative messages, there is no shortage of self-sabotaging beliefs that are interpretations disguised as facts. This exercise helps clients differentiate interpretations from facts.

T.I.P. #35 Worksheet: Fact Versus Fiction

IMPLEMENTATION: This activity is especially helpful with clients whose negative self-talk leads to excessive anxiety and depression. Explain to the client that we often treat our irrational interpretations about ourselves as facts, rather than see them for what they are—mere interpretations. Generate a list with your client or have him/her do this at home as a self-help assignment, helping to distinguish fact from interpretation.

PROCESSING: In going over the completed worksheet, reinforce the importance of separating fact from fiction in self-interpretations. Emphasize that this negative self-talk is simply not true so perhaps consider not giving these messages so much power!

FACT VERSUS FICTION

Interpretation	Fact
(example)	
I am awful at talking to people.	*I feel uncomfortable with others at times.*
My co-workers do not like me.	*A few of my co-workers do not talk to me.*
_____	_____
_____	_____
_____	_____
_____	_____
_____	_____
_____	_____
_____	_____

T.I.P. #36
"SHOULD" BUSTING ACTIVITY

THEORY: It is all too common to be under the "Tyranny of the Shoulds" (phrase taken from psychologist Karen Horney). This simple activity helps clients recognize and give up their "shoulds" in a visual, symbolic way. Instead of talking and thinking about it, they experience the act of relinquishing these toxic messages in this activity.

IMPLEMENTATION: Talk with clients either individually or in group about the irrational "shoulds" they carry around, handicapping their self-esteem and life adjustment. Have a jar in your office and tape "shoulds" on it. (I actually have a ceramic jar on which I had this word engraved prominently, but taping a sign on with a self-adhesive label would suffice.) Then have clients write on 3 x 5 cards or slips of paper the "should" messages they would like to give up. This is especially good for those with low self-esteem, anxiety, and depression. If this is done in a group, have a ceremony where one by one clients put messages in the jar, having the choice to express aloud or not the "should" they are attempting to relinquish.

PROCESSING: Have clients discuss how life will be different if they indeed can surrender the "shoulds." Imagine what changes can happen in your life if the irrational expectations are less powerful. I have had clients come in asking to put notes in my "should jar," even before or long after this assignment.

Sample "Shoulds" that would be fitting to put in this jar . . .

I should be right at all times.

I should be admired and liked at all times.

Others should be more like me.

I should be above average; being average is like being a loser or failure.

My spouse, parents, etc. should be more sensitive and understanding.

I should be further along in my life.

T.I.P. #37
TURNING AROUND THE "SHOULDS" IN AN ACRONYM

THEORY: Internalized self-talk characterized by "shoulds" is a roadblock to healthy emotional functioning. This therapeutic acronym offers a healthy alternative to the unhealthy "shoulds."

IMPLEMENTATION: Go over the acronym and discuss how this message can provide more constructive ways of thinking. Brainstorm with clients how they can use this acronym and apply other words to it (example: S stands for "statements").

Stop

Holding

On to

Unwarranted

Longstanding

Destructive

Self-talk

PROCESSING: Discuss how this acronym reminder can help clients keep their "shoulds" under control rather than have the unhealthy "shoulds" control them! This is easier said than done, but these aids will provide some structure to clients' "should" recovery!

T.I.P. #38
DEFEATING THE "SHOULDS" AND WORRY

THEORY: This handout is especially helpful for clients with anxiety issues. They will agree that worry and obsessive thinking limit their ability to function with a "level head." This handout serves as a very tangible support to those recovering from excessive, unrealistic worry and "shoulds."

T.I.P. #38 Handout: Shoulds, Worry, and Other Negative Habits of Thinking

IMPLEMENTATION: Suggest to clients that this handout will serve as an aid in their quest to quell their anxiety producing thoughts. Especially in times of extreme anxiety and panic, some clients find that this handout helps them keep things in perspective. You might have clients circle or even just verbalize the one or two items that relate most to their situation. You might tell them that worrying is just like being in a rocking chair—it's quite a ride, but you end up in the same exact place!

PROCESSING: Explore with clients how this handout can help them with their own specific worries and "shoulds." Suggest they leave the handout in their briefcase, notebook, etc. so that it can be readily available as a reminder in times of severe anxiety.

SHOULDS, WORRY, AND OTHER NEGATIVE HABITS OF THINKING

THE "SHOULDS"

- Life should be fair.

- People should be courteous and understanding.

- I should be more or less . . .

- Things should work out the way I want.

- Cars should never break down.

- Traffic should never stall.

BELIEVING THAT WORRY IS HELPFUL

- For example, if a member of my family is ill, I may tell myself that I should worry about him and feel guilty if I don't.

DWELLING ON WHAT COULD HAVE BEEN OR SHOULD HAVE BEEN

- For example, if I argue with a member of my family, I might keep thinking about what I could have said or how the other person should have acted.

EXPECTING THE WORST

- For example, if I am to have surgery, I may expect terrible pain and a long recovery period. This type of belief can lead to a "self-fulfilling prophecy"—what we expect to happen does happen because we make it happen.

ASSUMING THAT A MINOR NEGATIVE EVENT PREDICTS A MAJOR, MORE MOMENTOUS ONE

- For example, if I am reprimanded by my boss once in six months, I may assume she does not like me, thinks I am doing a bad job overall, and may fire me!

ASSUMING THAT A BAD SITUATION IS HOPELESS AND WILL NEVER CHANGE

QUOTES TO "DESTRESS FOR SUCCESS!"

"Its not stress that kills us, it is our reaction to it."

—Hans Selye

* * *

"Stress is the spice of life."

—Hans Selye

* * *

"I haven't failed, I've found 10,000 ways that don't work."

—Thomas Edison

* * *

"Rule 1. Don't sweat the small stuff.
Rule 2. It's all small stuff.
Rule 3. If you can't fight or flee, then flow."

—Robert Elliot

* * *

"It does not matter how slowly you go, so long as you do not stop."

—Confucius

Destress for Success!

T.I.P. #39
MINI-LECTURE: THE SERENITY PRAYER APPLIED TO STRESS MANAGEMENT

THEORY: Basically our job as mental health clinicians is to help people discover the Serenity Prayer for themselves! How many difficulties arise when this very simple message is not heeded! Although the Serenity Prayer began as an Alcoholics Anonymous motto, it easily can be applied to all of us and to ordinary life struggles.

T.I.P. #39 Worksheet: Serenity Prayer

IMPLEMENTATION: This worksheet is used with clients who lose sight of this message and try to change what they have no control over. They end up being "stress carriers" rather than "stress managers." Beware of those that say they don't have much stress—they likely are too busy giving it to others! This worksheet serves as a reminder for clients about the importance of the "3 As." Common sense? Perhaps, but very hard to put into practice! As my clients often remind me—easier said than done!

PROCESS: Process with clients what makes it so difficult to follow the motto of the Serenity Prayer. What irrational messages are we holding on to? How would our lives be different if the motto were followed?

SERENITY PRAYER

"God grant me the serenity to accept the things I cannot change, the courage to change the things I can, and the wisdom to know the difference."

AAABCs of Stress Management

ALTER: Problem-solving, direct communication, organizing, planning, time management, building up resistance, setting goals, changing your perceptions

AVOID: Walk away, let go, learn to say "no," delegate, set limits

ACCEPT: Let go of what you cannot change or control

What situations would I like to alter? _____

_____

_____

What situations can I avoid? _____

_____

_____

What situations do I need to accept? _____

_____

_____

T.I.P.s #40–#44
STRESS RESILIENCY

THEORY: These four handouts and one worksheet help clients develop hands-on skills for managing stress. T.I.P.s #40 through #44 offer various ways of developing skills to combat negative stress. They are ideal for Dialectical Behavior Therapy groups as well as for use with individual clients. Clients have kept them on their refrigerators, cars, etc. as reminders for dealing with life stress.

T.I.P. #40 Handout: Tips for Managing Stress

T.I.P. #41 Handout: Rules for Survival

T.I.P. #42 Handout: Tips for Emotional Resiliency

T.I.P. #43 Worksheet: Hardiness

T.I.P. #44 Handout: Resiliency Skills—Growing and Healing Through Change and Uncertainty

IMPLEMENTATION: The following materials are given to clients both in individual and group sessions. Items are gone over out loud until clients can relate items to their lives. I generally do not give out all these handouts at the same time but instead offer them on various weeks to bolster life skills education.

PROCESSING: These handouts are great not only for clients but for mental health staff for enhancing their ability to use skills in dealing with their own stresses, as well as in dealing with challenging clients!

TIPS FOR MANAGING STRESS

CHANGE TOXIC THOUGHT PATTERNS.

Attitudes such as, "I must be competent and a high achiever in every situation," are unrealistic. Sometimes people do not have conscious thoughts like this, but upon examination of behavior and attitude, find that they are holding themselves to a standard of absolute perfection. If these standards are not met, they feel like failures—they often grade themselves as 100% or "F."

ACCEPT AND MEET PHYSICAL AND PSYCHOLOGICAL NEEDS FOR EXERCISE, REST, GOOD NUTRITION, AND RECREATION.

Practice self-care techniques and attempt to nurture and nourish your body as well as your mind. Know your own physical limits and requirements and make them a priority. Be realistic on how to accomplish your goals.

DEVELOP A SENSE OF SELF-WORTH THAT IS NOT PRIMARILY DEPENDENT UPON SUCCESS, ACHIEVEMENTS, OR THE OPINIONS OF OTHERS.

There are two elements to our self-worth: an unconditional "no matter what" element, and a conditional "I must prove my self-worth by accomplishments and approval" element. Self-esteem too often is based on conditions that require the opinions and approval of others or your own high ideals. Wanting others to approve of you is not unhealthy, but often too much emphasis is placed on this.

ACCEPT IMPERFECTION, FAILURES, AND MISTAKES IN SELF AND OTHERS WITHOUT EXCESSIVE ANXIETY.

A healthy sense of self-worth helps balance inner critical voices. When there is an internal balance between self-worth and criticism, one often regards outside disapproval as a learning opportunity and a healthy challenge, despite the unpleasantness. One does not need to take a defensive posture, which is characterized by denying and attacking.

WELCOME FEELINGS, BOTH GOOD AND UNPLEASANT, AND LEARN TO COPE WELL WITH THE "BAD" ONES.

At times the best one can do with unpleasant feelings is to acknowledge them and accept them. Many times people deny their feelings, criticize themselves for feeling a certain way, and become defensive. This also makes it difficult to accept and acknowledge the feelings of others. Unpleasant feelings are normal and unavoidable, and are exacerbated when not allowed to be exposed.

DEVELOP GOOD, WARM, SUPPORTIVE RELATIONSHIPS.

Establishing good relationships with people—family, friends, co-workers, neighbors—can reduce stress immensely. Anyone who wants to develop a deep, mutually supportive relationship must take time to work on it, developing empathy, using self-disclosure to show the person "inside," expressing and dealing with feelings and emotions, and making a commitment to another person.

ONLY BY FOSTERING WELLNESS CONCEPTS IN OURSELVES CAN WE ACHIEVE A BETTER BALANCE IN OUR LIVES AND BE EMOTIONALLY OPEN AND AVAILABLE TO OTHERS.

RULES FOR SURVIVAL

RULE #1: DO NOT TAKE RESPONSIBILITY FOR THE THINGS YOU CANNOT CONTROL.

This can be only our own behavior, no one else's behavior. To be in control of our own behavior, we must recognize its limits.

RULE #2: TAKE CARE OF YOURSELF OR YOU CAN'T TAKE CARE OF ANYONE ELSE.

RULE #3: TROUBLE IS EASIER TO PREVENT THAN TO FIX.

RULE #4: BE ACCEPTING OF YOURSELF.

Don't ignore feelings and needs; accept limitations.

Limit the "tyranny of the shoulds."

RULE #5: BE ACCEPTING OF OTHERS.

Limit the "shoulds."

RULE #6: ASK FOR SUPPORT WHEN YOU NEED IT.

Seek people out who support you and use positive thinking skills.

RULE #7: ACCEPT, ALTER, OR AVOID A NEGATIVE SITUATION.

RULE #8: IF YOU NEVER MAKE MISTAKES, YOU'RE NOT LEARNING ANYTHING.

RULE #9: LIFE IS NOT FAIR OR A CONTEST.

Avoid the all-too-common "comparison trap."

RULE #10: ONE HAS TO BEGIN WHERE ONE IS.

TIPS FOR EMOTIONAL RESILIENCY

- *Focus on what you can control, not what's out of your control.* Be solution-focused, not problem-focused.

- *Use events as learning experiences.* The Chinese symbol for crisis is made up of the two symbols for danger plus opportunity. Be flexible and open-minded.

- *Alter your perceptions.* Don't try to change others! As Epictetus said in 1 A.D., "It is not events which disturb us, but our view of those events." Enhance rational thinking to prevent negativity from spinning out of control!

- *Limit the hostility factor.* The negativity and anger we harbor for others is more destructive to the one who harbors the resentment. Be generous and giving in spirit and avoid a negative focus.

- *Strive for GOODNESS, not PERFECTION!* Give up the need to be right. Limit defensiveness. Forgive—both yourself and others. Accept limitations. Let go of "shoulds," which make one bitter.

- *Develop compassion.* Choose kindness over being right. Resist the need to be critical.

- *Develop good self-care habits.* Allow yourself "mental health breaks" and "time out" regularly. Take care of needs in mind, body, and spirit. Eat well, exercise, and get enough sleep. Pamper yourself. Set limits, prioritize, and delegate.

- *Don't isolate yourself—CONNECT!* Avoid self-absorption. Seek to understand, not only to be understood.

- *Look for the humor in things.* Lighten up! Life is too serious to be taken too seriously. Accept that life isn't fair!

- *Develop mindfulness.* Learn to live in the present.

- *Don't ruminate on events that can't be changed.*

- *Accept the good as well as bad; neither will last forever.*

HARDINESS WORKSHEET

1. Identify a situation where you experienced distress: (Who? What? When? Where? Why?)

2. Alternatives

Think of three ways you could make the situation worse:	*Why didn't (or wouldn't) you do that?*
1.	1.
2.	2.
3.	3.

3. Exercise: Think of three ways you could make the situation better. What would you need to do to learn to handle the situation differently?

Better ways?	*Need to do or learn?*
1.	1.
2.	2.
3.	3.

95

RESILIENCY SKILLS

Growing and Healing Through Change and Uncertainty

USE FLEXIBLE THINKING SKILLS IN DEALING WITH UNCERTAINTY; SEE THE OPPORTUNITIES.

Instead of looking at the glass as half empty, look at the glass as half full. From adversity comes opportunity to change, to grow, to connect with others in a way you might not have connected before. Change and growth can be exciting and make one feel energized. Allow yourself to learn and heal in times of change. Embrace change! Don't fight it!

SEE STRESS AS YOUR FRIEND!

Stress often is only thought of as negative, but stress also can be positive. Stress can be invigorating, such as when playing on a sports team or working hard to complete a project you are proud of! Work stress also can be positive, as it helps one grow and change, and forces one to learn new skills and think in creative ways. Differentiate between stress that works for you and stress does that does not!

FOCUS ON WHAT YOU CAN CONTROL, NOT WHAT YOU CANNOT CONTROL; DON'T TRY TO CONTROL THE UNCONTROLLABLE!

Too often in the face of uncertainty one feels one is at the mercy of fate or circumstance, with a complete sense of loss of control. It is important to realize and exercise control in taking steps to make improvements in your life, not just clinging to hope that things will change. Alter what you can control; accept what you cannot control (as stated in the Serenity Prayer); have the wisdom to know the difference. If change seems too overwhelming, break up tasks necessary for change into small steps and short-terms goals. Hope alone all too often is just delayed disappointment.

PERCEPTION IS IMPORTANT! CHANGE TOXIC THOUGHT PATTERNS.

In times of change, it is important to realize that it is the interpretation and attitude that we have that determines how changes affect us. For example, attitudes such as "I can't stand any more changes" are immobilizing and irrational. Replace absolutes with "change is difficult" or "I am upset about the changes." When you think in absolute, "over-catastrophizing" terms, rational and healthy coping skills escape you. Tackle the paralyzing and irrational thinking that undermines one's well-being. Calm you mind and clear it of "clutter."

DEVELOP A SENSE OF SELF-WORTH THAT IS NOT PRIMARILY DEPENDENT UPON SUCCESS, ACHIEVEMENTS, OR EVEN THE OPINIONS OF OTHERS.

Never make the mistake of defining yourself too much by any thing outside yourself. Your worth as a person should never be contingent on the perception that one needs a relationship, job, or material success to make them worthwhile as a person. Too often, a person feels too dependent on another person, job, or living situation to make him/her feel good about self, and feels he/she is "nothing" without that person, job, or situation. Any extreme dependency only sets a person up for severe disappointment. When an unconditional sense of self-worth is not present, a person is vulnerable to depression and anxiety that is beyond his/her control.

BEWARE OF SUBSTANCE ABUSE!

In times of uncertainty, it is common to consume excessive alcohol or drugs. Escape and avoidance through chemicals except those prescribed and monitored by a physician never help one cope better and live a healthier life after the temporary "buzz" or "high" is gone. Impaired judgment, a sense of loss of control, and bad decision-making are some of the consequences. Healing one's pain by substance abuse invariably begets more pain, dysfunction, and bad choices.

ACCEPT AND MEET PHYSICAL AND PSYCHOLOGICAL NEEDS FOR EXERCISE, REST, GOOD NUTRITION, AND RECREATION.

Practice self-care techniques and attempt to nurture and nourish your body as well as your mind. Know your own physical limits and requirements, and make them a priority. Be realistic on how to accomplish your goals. Exercise regularly.

WELCOME FEELINGS, BOTH GOOD AND UNPLEASANT, AND LEARN TO COPE WELL WITH THE "BAD" ONES.

At times, the best one can do with unpleasant feelings is to acknowledge them and accept them. Many times people deny their feelings, criticize themselves for feeling a certain way, and become defensive. This also makes it difficult to accept and acknowledge the feelings of others. Unpleasant feelings are normal and unavoidable, and are exacerbated when they are repressed. It is not easy, but people who do not judge their feelings and who learn to accept their own fears, doubts, and discomforts will have less stress and will ultimately enjoy their lives more.

SEEK PROFESSIONAL HELP

All too often, people feel it is a sign of weakness to seek counseling or to get help from a physician when they are over-stressed. It is not a weakness to get help; it shows strength and courage to realize that help is needed. Personalized "coaching" on dealing with uncertainty can make a time of change and stress a very positive experience.

CONNECT, CONNECT, CONNECT!—DEVELOP GOOD, WARM, SUPPORTIVE RELATIONSHIPS.

Establishing supportive relationships is vital in stress resiliency. A sense that one is not alone and that one has important connections helps immensely in dealing with uncertainty. It is important not to keep your feelings in, and talking to others in a mutual give-and-take relationship can help one become more stress resilient. Do not use a time of severe stress to isolate yourself!

HUMOR AND LAUGHTER HELP!

No matter how stressful things can be, do not forget to laugh or use your sense of humor; it can help get you through! Too often with change and stress people feel humorless and forget how to have fun. Nothing should rob you of that ability!

ONLY BY FOSTERING WELLNESS CONCEPTS IN OURSELVES CAN WE ACHIEVE A BETTER BALANCE IN OUR LIVES, RESIST IMMOBILIZING STRESS, AND BE EMOTIONALLY OPEN AND AVAILABLE TO OTHERS.

T.I.P. #45
THE FOUR "Cs" OF THE STRESS-HARDY PERSONALITY

THEORY: In the late 1970s, Suzanne Kobasa of the University of Chicago conducted an 8-year research study of AT&T executives during the break-up of the company. She was curious to see what personality characteristics weathered the stress the best. She depicted four characteristics that made some executives the most resilient under such upheaval—uncertainty, layoffs, etc.

T.I.P. #45 Worksheet: Hardiness Skills—The Four "Cs"

IMPLEMENTATION: There are Four Cs of the Stress Resilient Personality according to researcher Kobasa. In introducing this exercise to clients, first ask them to guess what the Cs stand for. There are many words beginning with C that would make sense. Then share the Four Cs according to Kobasa's research. On the worksheet, these four factors are highlighted, with opportunity to tailor the idea to one's own situation.

PROCESSING: In learning about the Four Cs and filling in the following worksheet, people become more aware of how to use these principles to make active changes in their own lives to become more "stress resilient."

HARDINESS SKILLS—THE FOUR "Cs"

Suzanne Kobasa of the University of Chicago depicted four factors of the Stress-Hardy Personality. In each of the following, write one or two ideas of how you can develop these factors in your own life.

COMMITMENT: Those who feel a sense of commitment have a sense of involvement in something outside of themselves. They, therefore, tend not to feel isolated but rather sense that their actions have a purpose toward a greater good.

Ways I can feel more "committed": _____

_____

_____

CONTROL: This is perhaps the key factor in emotional health—a sense that you can control the things you can, but that does not mean controlling others! Rather than feel a victim of circumstance or a pawn in the lives of others, stress-hardy people feel an internal focus of control, in which they are the ones that "make things happen."

Ways I can feel more "in control": _____

_____

_____

CHALLENGE: In the face of adversity, people feel challenged and not overwhelmed. They view themselves as able to take on adversity rather than be flattened beneath the wheels of adversity. They are growth oriented and eager to meet new challenges.

Ways I can feel more challenged: _____

_____

_____

CONNECTION: People who feel a sense of connection with others, who do not feel isolated, tend to find support for their stress resilience. Those who isolate themselves and have a sense of alienation often do not fare as well in the face of adversity.

Ways I can feel more connected: _____

_____

_____

QUOTES FOR PERSONAL GROWTH

"If a man would move the world, he must first move himself."

—Socrates

* * *

"You'll never be on the top of the world if you try to carry it on your shoulders."

—Unknown

* * *

"What lies behind us and what lies before us are tiny matters compared to what lies within us."

—Ralph Waldo Emerson

* * *

"People are just as happy as they make up their minds to be."

—Abraham Lincoln

* * *

"Yesterday is history, tomorrow is a mystery, but today is a gift. . . . That's why they call it the present!"

—Eleanor Roosevelt

Self-Discovery and Growth

T.I.P. #46
ACTIVITY: WAKE UP AND SMELL THE COFFEE

THEORY: This hands-on activity is fun and takes very little time, but the lesson packs a punch! Who would think that a coffee filter could teach us about positive thinking? This visual activity shows us that no matter how down we feel, things are looking up!

IMPLEMENTATION: Provide one flat-bottomed coffee filter for each participant. Ask participants to write on the bottom side of the filter those negative self-talk messages that they persistently use with themselves. On the top side, ask them to write the healthier, counter-messages to those negative self-talk ideas. Then have them stand up and drop the filter. They find with surprise that the coffee filter winds up right-side up! How can we "right ourselves" and persist in more healthy patterns of thought? Another point to be made with this activity is that when we drop the filters from a sitting position, they often do not have enough time to right themselves. This illustrates the point that with the assumptions people make for themselves that help them remain pessimistic, they simply are not giving themselves enough time to "right themselves," so don't give up trying just yet!

PROCESSING: I have used this activity with clients, in training groups, and in workplace-wellness groups. No matter what the forum, people enjoy the activity and find the analogy quite useful. This is a popular favorite and one that reveals a profound message in a fun and active way. For extra punch, use huge industrial coffee filters. (I got them from a hotel at which I was doing a seminar.) The big filters work the same and make quite a sight!

T.I.P. #47
ACTIVITY: SELF-WORTH— WE'RE ALL ON THE "SAME PAGE"

THEORY: This is a visual demonstration that you can use in group or individual counseling. It demonstrates that our self-worth remains the same despite the traumas we go though or how inadequate we feel.

IMPLEMENTATION: Using a piece of paper, show a full piece and state that we begin life with a potential of wholeness in regard to self-esteem. So many of us, however, are then bombarded with many unhealthy and invalidating messages, such as that we are "bad." At this point, tear a piece of paper off the full piece. We then get the message that we are "selfish"; rip off another piece of paper. Then there is loss, family fragmentation, etc.; continue to tear off pieces of paper with each word spoken. We can keep shredding until we are left with a remnant—depending on how many "insults upon injury" one receives, one could be walking around with just a shred of self-confidence (demonstrated by the small remaining paper remnant). We can, however, tape these pieces back to make a whole; while there might be imperfections, they can all be saved. How much of a whole piece are you left with at present? How much can you put back together? Supply tape so the client(s) can put the pieces back together.

PROCESSING: This is a great visual representation of how we all begin on the "same page" but, depending on life events and our attitudes toward them, our self-esteem can be whittled away. As demonstrated, it can be salvaged and pieced back together like a puzzle. Although severe "life lines" and imperfections might be evident, these give our lives character, and we can learn to feel more whole.

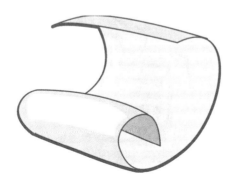

T.I.P. #48
ACTIVITY: MIRROR, MIRROR, ON THE WALL

THEORY: All too often, I have heard clients express, "I look in the mirror and do not like what I see." This exercise helps clients confront and analyze what they do see and hopefully learn to view themselves more positively.

IMPLEMENTATION: Have a client look in the mirror in your office and describe what he/she sees. Write down what the client says. Usual responses focus on what is on the outside, not the inside, and generally clients tend to focus on things about their appearance that can be changed. Point out this exact point, and address ways in which they can work on changing some of their dislikes. For instance, if a client is negative about hair looking too wavy, ask the client about ways in which he/she can make his/her hair straighter (e.g., go to a different hair stylist, try other products, use a flat iron). Also point out that they are looking outside for inner beauty. Isn't there more to them?

Next, after the client has had time looking in the mirror, ask who he/she most admires. Ask the client to write five characteristics of that person. Often this list is more focused on inner qualities than outer qualities. Compare this to the client's list for self, and offer the suggestion that perhaps he/she needs to look to his/her own inner qualities like he/she does for others.

PROCESSING: Point out to clients that they often are harder on themselves than others. They kindly and more gently look under the surface for others' positive qualities. But with themselves, they often are more punitive and focus too heavily on their exaggerated dislike of physical characteristics, which often can be changed to some degree anyhow.

T.I.P.s #49 & #50
"ROAD TO NOWHERE" AND "ROAD TO PARADISE"

THEORY: All too often we persist in entertaining self-defeating thoughts and behaviors that are not constructive and are not pointing us in a positive direction. These worksheet activities help identify particular thoughts and behaviors leading to "nowhere" or to "paradise."

T.I.P. #49 Worksheet: Caution—Road to Nowhere!

T.I.P. #50 Worksheet: Road to Paradise!

T.I.P. #49 IMPLEMENTATION: Use the "Caution—Road to Nowhere" worksheet with the client in session or as a self-help assignment to be completed as homework and shared in the following session. Ask the client to pick out main themes in thinking and behaving that are unhealthy and nonproductive that they meet up with often on their private "Road to Nowhere." The client's real-life examples help guide this activity.

T.I.P. #50 IMPLEMENTATION: Do not leave this activity without giving the client the option to make headway on the "Road to Paradise" and away from "Nowhere." Brainstorm how to turn the negative into the positive.

PROCESSING: These activities help clients uncover what behaviors and thoughts they persist in holding on to. Clients then are reminded visually through the worksheets that negative thoughts and behaviors lead only to nowhere—fast! Allow clients to see that they are at a crossroads in life . . . which path will they choose? . . . how can they journey to "paradise" and leave "nowhere" behind?

Caution—Road to Nowhere!

UNHEALTHY THOUGHTS: _____

_____

_____

_____

_____

_____

_____

UNHEALTHY BEHAVIORS: _____

_____

_____

_____

_____

_____

_____

_____

Road to Paradise!

HEALTHY THOUGHTS: _____

_____

_____

_____

_____

_____

_____

HEALTHY BEHAVIORS: _____

_____

_____

_____

_____

_____

_____

_____

T.I.P. #51
GIVING UP THE REARVIEW MIRROR SYNDROME

THEORY: All too often we focus on the past instead of being mindful and aware of our present. This poem and worksheet help clients look at the self-defeating "woulda, coulda, shoulda" messages that impede life.

T.I.P. #51 Worksheet: Giving Up the Rearview Mirror Syndrome!

IMPLEMENTATION: After clients fill out the worksheet, go over responses together. Process with clients how life would be different if they gave up the habit of living in the world of old images and photos. What is holding them back from being more focused on today rather than yesterday? Yesterday cannot be changed, so in focusing upon it, all sense of empowerment and control is lost and depression often pervades one's thoughts.

PROCESSING: In creating a new life picture album when we stop living so much in the past or in the future, we can experience the present more fully. As the saying goes, the past is a great place to visit, but you don't want to live there!

> *Yesterday is history, tomorrow is a mystery, but today is a gift . . . . That's why they call it the present!*
>
> —Eleanor Roosevelt

GIVING UP THE REARVIEW MIRROR SYNDROME

Woulda, coulda, shoulda
If only thinking . . .
You feel sad or depressed often
You try to re-write history
You think it's too late to change
You spend too much time in the past

Write your top two thoughts in each category:

Thoughts of things I "woulda" done: _____

_____

Thoughts of things I "coulda" done: _____

_____

Thoughts of things I "shoulda" done: _____

_____

Transform these regrets into self-help goals:

How much does forgiveness of self and others play into my reworking of old issues? _____

_____

_____

How can I focus on what is in my control instead of what is not? _____

_____

_____

_____

T.I.P. #52
BAGGAGE CHECK!

THEORY: We figuratively carry a lot of old emotional baggage around with us. Though perhaps invisible, it can weigh a ton! This worksheet can help clients conceptualize and identify the baggage that is weighing them down in their daily lives.

T.I.P. #52 Worksheet: Baggage Check

IMPLEMENTATION: Ask clients to fill out what unresolved issues and old messages weigh them down and cause difficulties. These issues can be a result of "shoulds" and expectations, or they might be in the form of disappointments or a sense of failure for a road not taken. Ask the client what they can do to lighten the load, how they can keep what they need but give up the rest that is impeding going forward.

PROCESSING: How would it feel to lighten your load? How would your life be different? This worksheet helps clients identify the individual ties and messages that weigh them down. One client claimed she literally would tote around a heavy backpack and once she "freed herself" of the need to be perfect and exorcised some inner demons, the need for the backpack—literally and figuratively—dissipated. She then could "lighten her load."

BAGGAGE CHECK

Old baggage refers to things in the past that cannot be changed, but interferes with present functioning. We all have baggage—the key is how you deal with it! Write what is in your baggage . . .

T.I.P. #53
ACTIVITY: KEEPING TRACK OF TIME

THEORY: Through use of a timeline, the client can better understand and explain present thoughts and behavior. A timeline can put one's life in perspective and validate why one has developed certain patterns of thought and behaviors. This exercise is great for Dialectical Behavior Therapy groups—exploring ways to promote client validation. If someone grows up needing to develop survival skills to get through a toxic family environment, for example, no wonder that person would choose survival over change!

IMPLEMENTATION: In this activity, client and therapist together make a timeline about various events in the client's life. This involves simply drawing a long horizontal line on a piece of paper and marking significant events in the client's life. This can be cathartic and can disarm defenses as the client acknowledges what obstacles in life he/she has survived. The clinician can point out that when one is in survival mode they do "get by," but healthiness also requires an ability to change and grow, which is often counter to a "survival" mentality.

PROCESSING: The therapist validates: "No wonder you needed to develop these survival skills! Most people would have handled it like that also, but now these skills are no longer adaptive." This type of activity can help a client learn to become "unstuck" from that defensive mode and move into a change-orientation.

T.I.P. #54
GROUP ACTIVITY: COLD PRICKLIES AND WARM FUZZIES

THEORY: When children are taught about how to get along with others at school, the concept of giving "cold pricklies" and "warm fuzzies" sometimes is used. This concept goes back to Alvyn Freed's book *T.A. for Tots* (1973). As we get older, how we forget the lessons of the cold pricklies and warm fuzzies! It is all too common for people to give off more cold pricklies than they realize. How? By using non-assertive and aggressive communication, they fail to deliver messages of warmth and tolerance.

IMPLEMENTATION: Explain the concept of the "cold pricklies" and "warm fuzzies." This is a great concept to employ when dealing with children or adults. Discuss the differences one feels in response to cold pricklies versus warm fuzzies. Brainstorm with clients their communications of the last couple of weeks where they both gave and received warm fuzzies or cold pricklies. Allow a couple minutes for each member to write down at least two of each category that he/she would feel comfortable discussing with the group, and ask for volunteers to share answers. The group can end this exercise by asking each member to think of one warm fuzzy he/she can give to another in the group, or to a special person in his/her life outside of the group.

PROCESSING: This makes individuals more likely to be in tune with the messages, both positive and negative, that they give to others. It helps people become aware of the importance of giving positive messages and helps them discriminate between the main types of messages we give and receive.

T.I.P. #55
SENTENCE COMPLETION

THEORY: This sentence completion worksheet is particularly helpful for a non-verbal client, for the very dependent client who needs some help beginning to express himself/herself, or for any client who has trouble expressing feelings. This is also valuable with children who might not have much to say but with some structure can share a lot.

T.I.P. #55 Worksheet: Sentence Completion

IMPLEMENTATION: The sentence completion worksheet can be used either as a self-help homework assignment or in session to elicit discussion topics. This is especially helpful for the very resistant or dependent client who needs structure to open up. The beginning of the sentence triggers ideas that can help to lead to participation and self-disclosure. I used this recently with a schoolteacher who was so frustrated and upset about events at school that she clammed up and felt immobilized with emotion, and only opened up when given the first part of a sentence for her to complete the rest.

PROCESSING: The sentence completion concept can provide very useful information about the client, and it often helps structure the therapeutic interview. This is just another tool for the toolbox to aid client self-expression.

SENTENCE COMPLETION

1. I enjoy _____

2. I am confused about _____

3. My favorite activity is _____

4. My greatest wish is _____

5. What makes me special is _____

6. I am unhappy about _____

7. My father _____

8. My mother _____

9. Some people _____

10. Happiness _____

11. One thing that I have lost is _____

12. The best thing about my job (or school) is _____

13. At night _____

14. When I am alone _____

15. I would like to forgive _____

16. I wish others would see me as _____

17. Many times I have tried _____

18. I have been surprised about _____

19. The thoughts that are hard to let go are _____

20. My best trait is _____

T.I.P. #56
SELF-CARE CONTRACT

THEORY: The self-care contract promotes the idea that we are in control of our behavior, thoughts, and feelings and it is "okay" to take care of ourselves. All too often we neglect our own self-care. Clients are encouraged to realize that self-care is not "selfish." We need to take care of ourselves in order to take care of others. Remind clients of what the flight attendants invariably say when introducing pre-flight groundrules. They warn that in case there is a problem and the oxygen masks come down, those with small children put the masks on themselves before assisting children.

T.I.P. #56 Worksheet: Personal Self-Care Contract

IMPLEMENTATION: Have the client fill out the self-care contract between sessions to assess and reprioritize self-care habits. Go over with the client what was written, and brainstorm how to implement these changes. Remind the client not to expect too much at once and that at times we need to break a goal into smaller, more manageable steps.

PROCESSING: This worksheet can give a detailed roadmap for steps toward self-care, thus improving self-esteem and sense of empowerment. It encourages the client to focus on specific changes that are within his/her control, and supports the notion that it is okay to work on oneself and that there is hope!

PERSONAL SELF-CARE CONTRACT

Individualized Plans and Goals

AT WORK OR SCHOOL

Relationships

Performance

AT HOME

Relationships

Performance

THINKING SKILLS

Negative thoughts to eliminate

Positive thoughts to increase

EMOTIONAL RESILIENCE

Tips to emotionally cope

ORGANIZATION AND TIME MANAGEMENT SKILLS

Strategies

Delegate responsibilities

SELF-CARE

Nutrition

Hobbies, Interests

Exercise

Relaxation

Humor

Spiritual

Date: _____ Signature: _____

QUOTES FOR INTROSPECTION AND CATHARSIS

"All that we are is the result of what we have thought. The mind is everything. What we think, we become."

—Buddha

* * *

"If we practice an eye for an eye and a tooth for a tooth, soon the whole world will be blind and toothless."

—Mahatma Ghandhi

* * *

"The one who throws the stone forgets; the one who is hit remembers forever."

—Angolan Proverb

* * *

"The reason one writes isn't the fact he wants to say something. He writes because he has something to say."

—F. Scott Fitzgerald

* * *

"You cannot depend on your eyes when your imagination is out of focus."

—Mark Twain

Introspective and Cathartic Exercises

T.I.P.s #57 & #58
THERAPEUTIC EFFECTS OF LETTER WRITING

THEORY: Letter writing can be a powerful way to express oneself and resolve relationship issues, even if the person one writes to is deceased or if the letter is designed to never be sent. Letter writing provides the client opportunity to express thoughts and feelings so that hopefully he/she can let go of old messages, feelings, and grudges that hinder growth. By expressing thoughts and feelings on paper, one has the power to take internal scripts and past reruns from darkness to light by using letter writing as the medium.

T.I.P. #57 To Whom It May Concern

IMPLEMENTATION: If a client's anger and lack of forgiveness or trauma causes them to be "stuck," letter writing provides a cathartic outlet. Many times these letters are not sent—they are vehicles to get out the anger and help the client embark on "letting go." The first step of letting go is not to deny but to acknowledge—to express the pain and give up the power it has on the present.

T.I.P. #58 The Crafted Letter

IMPLEMENTATION: After a client gets those unwanted old messages out, if he/she wants to actually send a letter to someone key in his/her life, the letter then is crafted by the therapist and client together to ensure it is a healthy letter. By carefully crafting well-chosen words, the client then has the greatest chance to be "heard!" Instruct the client not to expect a certain desired response. If the therapeutic goal is to express oneself, then the client can accomplish the goal without need of any "strings attached." If the response is favorable, it will then be a bonus.

PROCESSING: The use of letter writing can have a powerful effect in "letting go" and going through a grieving process of healing from the past.

T.I.P. #59
ACTIVITY: JOURNALING

THEORY: Journaling can elicit many important tools for the therapeutic relationship. A client can benefit from the cathartic effect of writing feelings and thoughts down, and also is less likely to forget to discuss certain thoughts if the journals are brought along to, and used, in the therapy session.

IMPLEMENTATION: I often have encouraged clients to use a journal to record and express feelings and thoughts. We use the journals in session to explore both constructive and destructive patterns of thinking. By identifying patterns of thoughts that create feelings, I have been able to reinforce cognitive therapy principles. Thus, patterns of thinking are detected, and negative self-talk can be addressed. Journaling also can serve as a way for clients to express themselves when there is not a support system in place for this. The cathartic effects of self-expression cannot be overstated.

PROCESSING: A client can use a journal to unleash thoughts and feelings so as not to "bottle them up." Journaling provides an excellent view into the internal mind of the individual—if it appears that the client is stuck in a particular way of thinking, reasons for the treatment resistance might become clearer. You also can use journaling in couples therapy so that each can grasp the other's issues in a way that previously had not been possible.

T.I.P. #60
WRITING MY EULOGY

THEORY: Living with an awareness of death does not have to be depressing. Rather, it can help clients reprioritize their actions in everyday life and jar them into getting their priorities straight in light of the fact that we do not come out of this world alive! In facing death and what we hope to be remembered for, we can better live our lives with our goals in mind.

IMPLEMENTATION: Have your client write his/her own eulogy. Although this might seem like a depressing assignment, it actually can turn morbidity into life affirming involvement. Ask your client, "what really is important to you?" "What would you like to be remembered for?" "How are your choices now in life reflecting your most lofty goals and priorities?" This can be a powerful exercise for clients who would benefit from self-exploration and insight into what really is important to them. This can be done in a group or individual setting, and in the case of a group, eulogies can be read aloud and reactions shared. In individual treatment, the client can read the eulogy to the counselor and then brainstorm how he/she can use the ideas expressed as goals to reprioritize his/her life. How can priorities be changed so as to incorporate the concepts from the eulogy?

PROCESSING: This powerful exercise is not for the individual who is suicidal, but rather the individual who can benefit from self-discovery and self-awareness. Perhaps it might be the client who spends too much time fretting about the past or worrying about "what ifs" in the future.

T.I.P. #61
UNLEASHING THE POWER OF FORGIVENESS

THEORY: A lack of forgiveness is often the root of poor communication with individuals in one's life. All too often there is a lack of forgiveness for actions, words, and failed expectations. This focus on forgiveness in this exercise helps one let go of resentments that cause unproductive and self-destructive anger.

IMPLEMENTATION: I often use reframing in counseling for clients who harbor resentment and anger, whether these be directed toward family of origin or toward a current or estranged loved one. I ask clients, "are they bad or unhealthy?" Intentionality is then taken out of the equation; this question communicates the idea that perhaps if the person had a choice, he/she would not opt for such toxic behaviors. Most clients respond with, "unhealthy." It is easier to forgive someone for being unhealthy than for being bad. Judging and labeling then give way to empathy. I then ask if clients can forgive the person for not knowing any better, for being unhealthy. I nearly always get a resounding "yes."

This fundamental question is powerful for dealing with family of origin issues and in couples therapy when there is extreme discord, blame, and conflict. What was seen as despicable gets relabeled as "unhealthy," and the need to blame diminishes. This distinction posed by the therapist can redirect negative energy into positive energy!

PROCESSING: This ability to reframe and relabel transforms resentments into opportunities for growth. Forgiveness enables one to let go of resentments and blame, and helps one learn to accept what cannot be changed. This idea of forgiveness also can help the individual who is too hard on himself/herself and cannot forgive self for being anything less than perfect. Offer both others and yourself the olive branch!

"Forgiveness is the fragrance that the violet sheds on the heel that has crushed it."

—Mark Twain

"Forgiveness is giving up the possibility of a better past."

—Mahatma Ghandhi

T.I.P. #62
WEIGHING THE PROS AND CONS

THEORY: How often do we need to make a decision and are unsure of which way to go? How often are we faced with a crossroad of alternatives and feel paralyzed to make a choice? How often do we find ourselves stuck in an unhealthy relationship or situation but are not sure we want to give up the "known" for the "unknown?" This worksheet helps clients prioritize the "pros" and "cons" of a decision.

T.I.P. #62 Worksheet: Weighing the Pros and Cons

IMPLEMENTATION: The following worksheet can be given to a client who remains stuck in an unstable or unhealthy situation, or one who is unsure about a major life decision. The process of weighing out the pros and cons in a methodical way can be more enlightening than one might realize. It might sound obvious, but seeing the two alternatives on paper offers an enlightening perspective!

PROCESSING: Help the client decide how to handle the information reaped from this exercise. Timing, of course, has to be right. One might clarify direction but still need help in being strong enough to carry through with a decision. Whatever the timing, goals of counseling often become clearer after carefully weighing the pros and cons.

WEIGHING THE PROS AND CONS

The situation I am concerned with is: _____

_____

The Pros to staying in this situation are: *The Cons to staying in this situation are:*

_____   _____

_____   _____

_____   _____

_____   _____

In comparing the two lists, what do I notice? _____

_____

Put a number from 1 to 5 next to the "weightiness" of each idea.

Add up your numbers for each idea.

Total number for Pros is _____

Total number for Cons is _____

Based on my lists and numbers, what inferences can I make? _____

_____

How might this help me in making a decision? _____

_____

What might interfere with or impede this decision? _____

_____

What steps will I want to take based on my "findings?" _____

_____

T.I.P.s #63–#65
PERSONAL LIFE STORIES

THEORY: We all have our "Stories." This activity encourages clients to review their lives and crystallize how they would sum up key points of their "life story." This review can help clients reflect on themes that shaped them into who they are and can help prioritize where they go from here.

T.I.P. #63 Activity: Life Story

T.I.P. #64 Activity: Joint History

T.I.P. #65 Group Activity: Who Is Yours Truly

T.I.P. #63 IMPLEMENTATION: Ask your client to reflect for a few minutes and make a title for his/her "life story" autobiography. What would be the most difficult chapter to write? What would be the most fun chapter to write? Who would be the most central characters throughout the book? Who do you wish you could leave out? What chapter would you love to include if it were true?

T.I.P. #64 IMPLEMENTATION: A variation on the life story idea is to ask a couple to envision a co-authored book—what would that title be? What would be their most difficult chapter? What would be the best chapter of their lives together? Ask, in your wildest imagination, what chapter would you love to include in your life together? How would perspective be different depending on who wrote certain parts? Would the emotional tone of various chapters be different between the two authors? Would you each choose different things to put in or leave out?

T.I.P. #65 IMPLEMENTATION: In a well-established group where members are acquainted with one another, have each person write on a 3 x 5 card a title of his/her life story. On the card, put the first chapter heading, a middle chapter heading, and the last chapter heading. Then put them in a hat or jar and have a designated person pull out the cards and read them aloud, the group then guessing who wrote each and why. This is a fun group activity and also a great way to learn more about one another.

PROCESSING: These Personal Life Stories activities can help clients summarize key feelings and thoughts about life's events, and fill in dreams, hopes, and goals in light of these realizations. Reviewing, prioritizing, and goal-setting can spur clients to make healthier life decisions in the present and future.

T.I.P. #66
FIVE STAGES OF GRIEVING

THEORY: The "five stages of grieving" by Elisabeth Kubler-Ross has long been the standard model for how people deal with loss. Even though originally these stages were conceptualized for facing death of a loved one or facing one's own mortality, the model can be very powerful for understanding the loss of a relationship, marriage, job, dream, or even just the illusion that you thought a person was someone he/she isn't. I use this handout often when dealing with clients who are depressed and/or suffering from the demise of a relationship, including marital breakup.

T.I.P. #66 Five Stages of Grieving

IMPLEMENTATION: This sheet has proved helpful for those struggling with many types of loss. Have a client identify what stages he/she has gone through and where he/she is stuck in grieving the loss. The loss can be a psychological loss as well as a "real-life" loss—such as the facing of one's aging and mortality. It might be breaking through denial and facing the reality that your spouse is not who you "hoped" he/she would be. Those going through a painful separation or divorce find this model extremely helpful in learning to grow into acceptance.

PROCESSING: It is unavoidable—we all go through stages of grieving when overcoming hurt and loss. That is a necessary part of life, as Judith Viorst explains in her book *Necessary Losses*. Only by leaving and being left, letting go and moving on, can we grow from inevitable loss and replace the loss with personal growth. If we do not choose growth, we will be immobilized from the loss and become "stuck." How painful it has been for so many people who have carried to their graves the incomplete mourning of losses in their lives, those who have never grown through to the final stage of acceptance.

FIVE STAGES OF GRIEVING

(based on teachings of Elisabeth Kubler-Ross)

5 Stages	Of Death and Dying	Of Healing a Memory
DENIAL	I avoid facing the likelihood of my death. I cannot face mortality. I feel and act as though I am invincible.	I don't admit I either am or ever was hurt. I don't face the reality of my unrealized dreams and illusions. I see things like I want to see them, and not as they are.
ANGER	I blame others for letting death hurt and destroy me. I am filled with resentment and can't forgive.	I blame others for hurting and destroying me. Others are responsible for my pain, and I can't forgive. Anger and "shoulds" consume me.
BARGAINING	I set up conditions to be fulfilled before I'm ready to die. If I do, then I can avoid reality and make things as I want to be.	I set up conditions to be fulfilled before I'm ready to forgive others and myself. If I act in a certain way, perhaps I can get others to change their minds or behaviors.
DEPRESSION	I blame myself for letting death take over. I failed in my life—I didn't accomplish what I had hoped—I have much regret.	I blame myself for letting hurt destroy me. I failed and am powerless, ashamed, and helpless. Hopelessness, regret, and despair consume me.
ACCEPTANCE	I'm ready to die. I've made peace with others and myself. I have come to terms with my mortality.	I look forward to growth from hurt and change. I can accept and forgive myself and others. I can let go of impossible dreams, illusions, "shoulds," and expectations without a veil of delusion.

131

T.I.P. #67
ACTIVITY: IDENTIFYING CHARACTERISTICS OF THE DYSFUNCTIONAL FAMILY

THEORY: This is an enlightening activity to explore characteristics and interaction patterns of troubled families. Ask clients if they can identify with any of these family roles.

T.I.P. #67 Handout: Family Roles in the Dysfunctional Family

IMPLEMENTATION: Brainstorm characteristics of dysfunctional families on a flipchart. Caution that this activity is not meant to blame but solely to understand that "people do the best as they can." Objectifying how one's family was dysfunctional can help one set oneself free from the toxic effects of that family.

Possible Characteristics for the Flipchart

Violent	Exploitive	Disturbed interactions
Unclear roles	Authoritarian	Addictive
Deprives	Low self-worth	Invalidating
Double bind	Abusive	Invisible loyalties
Leads to low self-esteem	Homeostasis	Martial discord
Addicted	Enmeshment	Non-assertive or aggressive
Pseudomutuality	Leads to helplessness and vulnerability	

It might be helpful to talk about the four general child roles of the troubled family—the "Hero" (the one who survives and excels), the "Mascot" (the one who uses humor and joking to cope with the pain), the "Scapegoat" (the symptoms are bound and focused on one individual who is regarded as "bad"), and the "Lost Child" (who ends up with low self-esteem and self-sabotaging behavior, such as drug and alcohol use).

PROCESSING: In understanding the dysfunction objectively, one can work on freeing oneself from the toxic effects of an unhealthy and painful family legacy. Exploration of these concepts in a group setting provides a sense of universality—that one is not alone—and offers communal strength to participants.

FAMILY ROLES IN THE DYSFUNCTIONAL FAMILY

 *Hero—*

 *Scapegoat—*

 *Mascot—*

 *Lost Child—*

QUOTATIONS FOR COUPLES

"There is no more lovely, friendly, and charming relationship, communion, or company than a good marriage."

—Martin Luther King

* * *

"Before marriage, many couples are very much like people rushing to catch an airplane; once aboard, they turn into passengers. They just sit there."

—Paul Getty

* * *

"Relationships are like crystals, you don't realize how much you love it until it breaks."

—Unknown

* * *

"Consider how hard it is to change yourself and you'll understand what little chance you have in trying to change others."

—Unknown

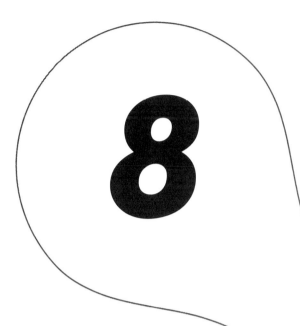

Couple Considerations

T.I.P. #68
ROLE-PLAY VARIATIONS WITH COUPLES

THEORY: One of the most effective strategies I have found for working with couples is the use of role-play. In transitioning to role-play quickly and naturally without much "ado," I avoid the common groans and moans about "acting" in a role-play. Through role-play, clients get a chance to observe and change their styles of communication and learn to actively listen to one another.

IMPLEMENTATION: It is not unusual to observe couples in my office talking "at" one another rather than "with" one another. In trying to get across one's own point of view, often one or both individuals are "on the defensive," trying to get their point across but not really "listening" to the other. I demonstrate to them how they came across by playing one of the spouses at a time. I ask how accurate my imitation was and how it sounded—usually the client agrees that he/she indeed does not sound as good as he/she had thought! Then, I role model active listening techniques as in T.I.P.s #12 and #13, after which I give clients a chance to follow my lead. Even though it is an "artificial" role-play, where at times they even copy my exact words (as they do not yet think in that way!), it is not uncommon for a client to become tearful or sob after hearing the spouse talk in a tender way that a client may never have heard before!

An interesting variation includes having the spouses play one another. You are bound to have quite a fun, lively, "perspective altering" interchange!

PROCESSING: The role-play becomes "real" in a very short period of time. This has provided me with an opportunity to teach hands-on communication and listening skills, which has been especially helpful when combining the role-play experience with handouts on communication and listening skills (see T.I.P.s #3, #4, #12, and #13).

T.I.P. #69
LETTER WRITING FOR COUPLES

THEORY: When focusing on improving marital communication, sometimes deep-seated feelings and thoughts need thoughtful expression. This letter writing activity in couple therapy gives opportunity for that expression of feelings.

IMPLEMENTATION: In some situations, even after role-plays and discussion of a couple's communication patterns, one or the other in the couple still does not feel "heard" and "understood." In these cases, instruct a couple to write letters to one another about their feelings and not to show the letters to one another until reading them aloud in the next session. If a client fails to do the assignment, that is providing important information right there! If one writes a long note and the other a very simple, hastily-composed letter, you have more information to work with on the differences in motivation for each individual. Let the clients know, "The goal is to get your feelings out, not to change the other person."

PROCESSING: Clients can share their reactions to writing and hearing the other's letter. Discuss: Did processing on paper help in expressing difficult emotions? Letters can be kept in the counseling office and given to the clients later on for perspective.

T.I.P.s #70 & #71
STRATEGIES FOR COUPLES

THEORY: These exercises are aimed at diminishing the power of the right/wrong mentality and giving way to a "we" mentality. In the case of a couple, letting the other be right or letting the other have the last word can be more tolerable than imagined—with the correct attitude! These activities have at their base the concept that a "We" mentality is the foundation for "Wellness," and an "I" mentality underlies "Illness."

T.I.P. #70 Let the Other Be Right for a Change!

IMPLEMENTATION: If I could think of one persistent problem at the heart of couple difficulties, it is the nagging fear that one partner is right and the other wrong! This activity forces a client to go to the other extreme—looking for ways that the partner is right! If you have witnessed in a couple's communication the inflexible need to be "right" and "righteous," this activity can make for an interesting and amusing session. Point out to the couple that the need to be right might be helping the "I" but not the "We." Ask them to find three instances where one was wrong and the other was right. Have the couple face each other and share three examples of when the other was the "right" one.

T.I.P. #71 Let the Other Have the Last Word!

IMPLEMENTATION: In this fun exercise, couples who are prone to arguing are each instructed to let the other have the last word. This tends to keep them on better behavior in no time! This exaggeration of communication makes it difficult to keep on spouting off, since the idea of the activity is to pave the way for the other to be expressive. Learning to not have the last word might at first create anxiety—and perhaps some silence—when tried at home, but teaches a great lesson in listening and patience.

PROCESSING: Explore with the couple how it felt to "admit" they were wrong and how they felt each accepting the other's behavior as "right." What they have been fighting against all along—the need to be right—was perhaps not so important after all.

T.I.P. #72
DEMONSTRATION: ILLNESS VERSUS WELLNESS

THEORY: These demonstrations allow couples to evaluate how their "I" focus has been at the expense of the "We" focus of teamwork.

IMPLEMENTATION: Draw a diagram of two circles overlapping in the middle. Each circle represents one of the clients, and the inner overlapping oval represents the "Team" concept of the "We." Brainstorm with clients how many of their thoughts and behaviors are at the service of the "I" in their own circles and how many are focused on the teamwork that the overlapping oval represents.

PROCESSING: Discuss: What can they change to put more focus on the "We?" Boundaries are important, but if the boundaries are too rigid and the "I" takes precedence over the "We," the relationship will suffer. Conversely, too much enmeshment and co-dependency and not enough individuality also can be stifling. Brainstorm with clients practical ways they can strengthen the relationship as well as maintain healthy boundaries where they are not parasitic on one another but also not each in his/her "own world."

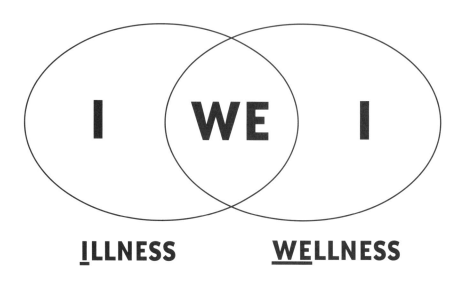

T.I.P. #73
MINI-LECTURE:
THE 90/10 PRINCIPLE

THEORY: I often teach clients the simple concept of the 90/10 principle—90 percent of what you are arguing about is not what you are arguing about. All too often, clients do not remember the origin of a given argument for this reason—90 percent is not about that. The argument was just a trigger for unresolved dreams, expectations, disappointments, and so on.

IMPLEMENTATION: Discuss this theory with clients and encourage them not to get sidetracked by the 10%!

PROCESSING: Discuss: When you keep the 90/10 principle in mind and choose not to get lost in the 10, how does it feel to be focusing on the good of the "We" instead of the "I?" Why is the "I" often so difficult to give up? Or, conversely for a client needing to break the habit of co-dependency, why is the "I" so difficult to uphold? As couples work through and gain insight from the T.I.P.s in this chapter, it will be more difficult for them to repeat the same pattern, knowing it is not in the best interest of the "we."

T.I.P. #74
SECOND CHANCE ROLE-PLAYS FOR COUPLES

THEORY: This exercise empowers clients to learn from "mistakes." People often learn more from mistakes than successes, though all too many are immobilized by mistakes rather than treating them as learning opportunities. This exercise indeed gives couples a "second chance."

IMPLEMENTATION: Have the couple talk about a situation that they handled in a non-productive or disappointing way. Role-play the situation in the office, where you can coach the clients on how to act differently in the scenario. You might role model the behavior for the clients, playing one or both of the clients at different times to offer communication ideas. Then switch roles and have the clients play themselves, handling the situation in a better way. Thus, the couple is instilled with hope that they have learned from this and will have better skills for the future—a second chance!

PROCESSING: This exercise reminds us that we can use setbacks as learning opportunities and be forward-looking instead of wallowing in disappointment. This second chance, hopefully, can transfer to future situations. This exercise can prove inspiring, giving hope to couples who might be on the brink of separation or divorce, reminding them of the possibility of a "second chance."

QUOTES ON BEHAVIORAL AND EXPERIENTIAL STRATEGIES

"An idea that is developed and put into action is more important than an idea that exists only as an idea."

—Buddha

* * *

"Remember, people will judge you by your actions, not your intentions. You may have a heart of gold, but so does a hard-boiled egg."

—Unknown

* * *

"Physical fitness is not only one of the most important keys to a healthy body, it is the basis of dynamic and creative intellectual activity."

—John F. Kennedy

* * *

"The happiness of a man in this life does not consist in the absence but in the mastery of his passions."

—Alfred, Lord Tennyson

* * *

"It is folly for a man to pray to the gods for that which he has the power to obtain by himself."

—Epicurus

9

Behavioral and Experiential Strategies

T.I.P. #75
WORKOUT LOG FOR MENTAL FITNESS

THEORY: Many people would not think twice about having a fitness log for their workout or exercise routine but would not consider applying the same concept to their "mental fitness" training. A therapist might act as a "coach" for "mental fitness" just as one would hire a personal trainer for weight training. Having a fitness plan in writing can help structure change in developing better self-care habits.

T.I.P. #75 Worksheet: Mental Fitness Log

IMPLEMENTATION: This worksheet provides a structure for tailoring a client's "mental fitness" regimen. By breaking goals into manageable steps (similar to increasing weights gradually in weight training), one can see small improvements toward a greater goal. This helps provide motivation and can keep personal commitment fresh! As "coach," review your client's fitness log each session and help fine-tune goals and expectations. Reinforce positive steps taken, and help the client discern which aspects of his/her program might be neglected or might be causing concern.

PROCESSING: This matter-of-fact approach is comprised of concrete, practical steps toward self-empowerment. This also underscores the point that "mental fitness" is just as important as "physical fitness"!

MENTAL FITNESS LOG

	SUN.	MON.	TUES.	WED.	THURS.	FRI.	SAT.

Goals for the Month—Steps to Take:

Organizing Myself: Workspace
                       Bedroom
                       Home
                       Kitchen

Exercise: Weight training
              Walking
              Gym classes
              Other

Food Habits: Organize food at home
                 Shop for healthy choices
                 Cook on weekends/healthy alternatives
                 Diminish use of "fast foods"

Journal: Write in journal

Connecting: Reconnect with old friends
                Call a friend
                Initiate a social activity

Hobbies: Spend time on hobby

Try a new activity:

Use assertive skills: At home
                          At work
                          With children
                          With parents

148

T.I.P.s #76–#78
BREAKING THE "BLUE MOOD? MORE FOOD" CYCLE

THEORY: Food addiction is increasingly common, and obesity rates in the United States continue to rise. These three T.I.P.s help clients understand how to gain more control of their eating habits and to feel empowered through insight and education to stop the "Blue Mood? More Food" cycle.

T.I.P. #76 Handout: How to Halt an Unproductive Relationship with Food

T.I.P. #77 Handout: Strategies for Developing Good Food Habits

T.I.P. #78 Worksheet: Food/Mood/Thought Diary

IMPLEMENTATION: These strategies provide practical tips for helping clients give up the unhealthy habits of food addiction. Practical suggestions, insight into thinking habits, and the emphasis on empowering oneself in the areas of thought, mood, and behavior are addressed. These T.I.P.s lend structure to those needing practical strategies for breaking food addiction. After reading and discussing the first two handouts, the client then can use this background information to dissect his/her food/mood/thought patterns. Have the client come to the session prepared to show his/her diary. Then brainstorm alternatives to the thinking that triggers poor food choices.

PROCESSING: Explore with the client how the handouts and worksheet can provide structure and insight to defeat food addiction.

HOW TO HALT AN UNPRODUCTIVE RELATIONSHIP WITH FOOD

- Keep a food/mood/thought diary.

- Watch out for the "blue mood? more food" cycle.

- Enjoy new treats. Be creative in finding non-food rewards.

- Work on solving the real problem.

- Delay, distract.

- Reach out and touch someone—confide in others.

- Take a "time out."

- Practice safe snacking.

- Plan ahead.

- Feed your heart and nourish your soul.

- Use positive messages replacing self-criticism.

- Confide in others who are supportive.

- Listen and accept your feelings.

- Make time for self-reflection.

- Each setback is a learning experience.

- Get enough play in your life.

- Exercise, exercise, exercise!

- Bombard yourself with health/fitness magazines and books.

- Use moderation in everything.

- Use behavioral methods for "response prevention."

(Adapted from "Food and You" by *Prevention* magazine)

STRATEGIES FOR DEVELOPING GOOD FOOD HABITS

BEHAVIORAL

- Response prevention strategies

  —Keep the pantry stocked with nutritious choices of food.

  —Do not have foods around that cause problems for you.

  —Buy small.

  —Don't go places that will be too tempting.

  —Don't hover near food that is cooking; it will cook itself!

  —Keep tempting foods out of sight and off limits.

- Reinforce yourself with non-food rewards.

- Eat small meals throughout the day.

- Eat in the same place at home—not in the car, standing up, or in front of the TV.

- Quit the clean-plate club.

- Eat mindfully, slowly, and without distractions.

- Set small, realistic goals, and don't expect too much too soon!

- Have plenty of water and dilute drinks with water.

- Use small plates.

- Leave food on the stove—not on the table!

- Keep a food/mood/thought diary.

- Don't diet; have a lifestyle plan.

- Learn good stress management and communication skills.

- Read literature that is reinforcing and inspiring.

- Use relaxation, meditation, deep breathing, and visualization techniques.

- Exercise at least 20 to 30 minutes, at least four times a week.

EMOTIONAL

- Uncover reasons for emotional eating.

- Feed your heart, nourish your soul.

- Connect, look for love, and comfort, with others.

- Be close to nature.

- Get in touch with feelings.

- Accept all emotions non-judgmentally, not labeling them as "good" or "bad."

- Reach out.

- Express feelings.

- Heal resentments.

- Forgive.

- Find ways to enhance self-acceptance and self-esteem.

- Heal old wounds.

- Know your emotional triggers.

THOUGHT

- Think rationally; limit "all or nothing" thinking.

- Replace irrational beliefs with more rational beliefs.

- Don't "over-catastrophize."

- Appreciate the food/mood/thought connection.

- Determine reasons for emotional eating— peel back the skins of the onion.

- Decide consciously what to do about your food habits.

- Reevaluate old messages.

- Examine your associations with food, replacing old messages with new messages.

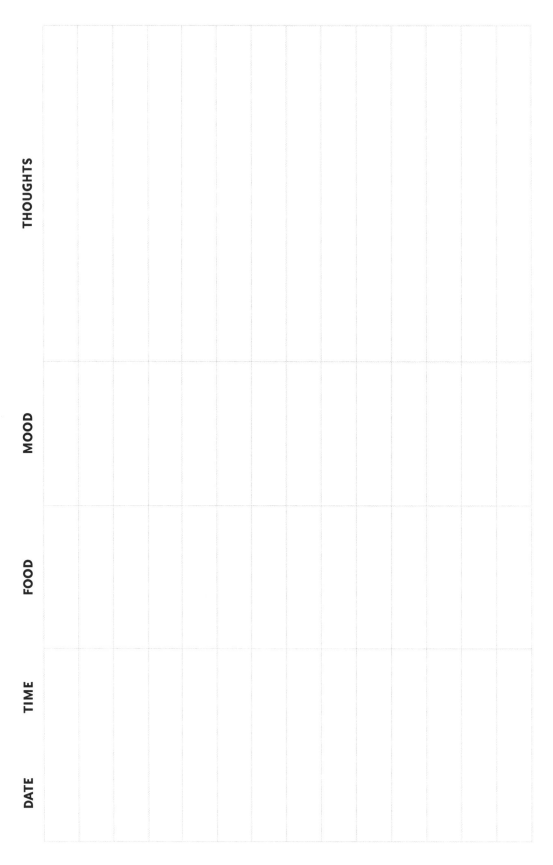

FOOD/MOOD/THOUGHT DIARY

DATE	TIME	FOOD	MOOD	THOUGHTS

T.I.P. #79
BEHAVIORAL CHARTING TO SHAPE BEHAVIOR

THEORY: What about a good old-fashioned behavioral chart for self-shaping a behavior? The concepts of operant conditioning are still in vogue with teachers and mental health professionals for helping students and clients shape more positive behavioral habits.

IMPLEMENTATION: Behavioral charts can be very effective in shaping behavior, and take emotion out of conflict. For example, a parent struggling with parent-child conflict hopefully can learn to replace yelling with self-control and a focus on providing natural and logical consequences to the child. In the case of adolescent or in-patient facilities, a behavioral chart where a resident earns privileges by doing certain behaviors can be very powerful indeed, especially when insight-orientation is not achievable, as with low functioning individuals. One also might use self-shaping charts to change one's own behavior, as in following a healthier food regimen to lose weight, or establishing an exercise plan and sticking with it. In this self-directed program, a client and therapist brainstorm rewards if goals are met.

PROCESSING: Follow up with clients as to how their programs are working for shaping and controlling their own behavior or their children's behavior. Does the chart and reward system make it easier to develop habits without resorting to frustration and yelling? Using a behavioral chart is a commonplace strategy in schools but one that is often overlooked in therapeutic settings when seeking to shape positive behavioral patterns.

BEHAVIOR CHART

(Using a Reward System)

Goal: *Buy myself the book I want after two weeks of success*

	SUN.	MON.	TUES.	WED.	THURS.	FRI.	SAT.
Say something nice to my co-worker twice each week.			✶			✶	
Walk four times weekly for 25 minutes.	✶		✶	✶		✶	
Speak up in a meeting twice each week.		✶			✶		

154

T.I.P.s #80–#82
STAND UP FOR YOUR RIGHTS!

THEORY: This handout and accompanying exercises enforce the idea that we all have a right to be treated with respect, and one person's rights are no less or more important than another's. Particularly for the co-dependent who is sacrificing continually for others, the message is conveyed that it is not "selfish" to pursue your own rights, as long as you keep in mind your corresponding responsibilities.

T.I.P. #80 Handout: Basic Human Rights

T.I.P. #81 Visual Imagery on Basic Human Rights

T.I.P. #82 Group Brainstorming Activity: You Have a Right to Have Rights!

T.I.P.#80 IMPLEMENTATION: Use the Basic Human Rights handout as a basis for discussion. Group members can take turns reading the items, or in the case of individual therapy, the therapist and client can takes turns reading all or just choose items pertaining most to the individual. Address the rights that clients have the most difficulty accepting for themselves. Brainstorm what holds them back. What messages are they carrying around that deny fundamental rights? Where did they get those messages? Do they objectively agree with it now? All too often, we relinquish our rights to others and then feel spent and misunderstood. This can be tied nicely to the handouts and exercises on assertiveness (T.I.P.s #10 and #11), as identification of basic human rights is essential in standing up to others assertively.

T.I.P. #81 IMPLEMENTATION: Have participants close their eyes and use guided imagery to imagine that they have one right that they would like to have and what life would be like if they had that right. How would life be different? What do they need to do to accept the rights they have so much trouble accepting in everyday life? How would they feel differently about themselves if they accepted that right? Now imagine if that right was taken away. How does that feel? How is life different now? Are there people in your life who do not feel you should have those rights? How can you express yourself to them and not feed into continued denial of those basic human rights?

T.I.P. #82 IMPLEMENTATION: In this exercise the group leader uses a flipchart or chalkboard and asks for rights that group members need to work on accepting. After making a column for this, have a column on the other side for corresponding responsibilities. To every right there is a corresponding responsibility. All too often, people give up their rights and defer to others who take advantage of their self-defacing actions. Clients may feel that it is selfish to stand up for a certain right. Emphasizing the corresponding responsibilities, however, underscores that one is still "responsible" even when addressing one's own needs, that it does not mean one is being "self-centered" or "selfish."

PROCESSING: These basic human rights handout and exercises can go very well with the assertiveness portion of this book but can stand alone as effectively enhancing self-esteem and empowerment. Clients welcome the notion that they are not being "selfish" simply by feeling that they have a "right" to have "rights."

BASIC HUMAN RIGHTS

1. The right to have and express your own feelings and opinions

2. The right to be treated with respect

3. The right to feel and express anger

4. The right to say "no"

5. The right to set your own limits and priorities

6. The right not to live up to other people's expectations of you

7. The right not to be "Superman," "Superwoman," "Superboss," "Supermother," etc.

8. The right to be treated with courtesy and respect

9. The right to ask for what you want and have your needs be as important as the needs of other people

10. The right to get what you pay for

11. The right to ask for help

12. The right to ask that others change their behaviors that violate your own rights and to have a preference about how others act

13. The right to make mistakes

14. The right not to be brilliant, attractive, slim, and witty

15. The right to privacy

16. The right to forgive yourself

17. The right to forgive others

18. The right to change your mind

19. The right to not feel responsible for others' feelings and behaviors

20. The right to choose not to assert yourself

T.I.P. #83
THE POWER OF ROLE-PLAY

THEORY: The use of role-play has been one of my favorite tools in individual treatment. Sometimes talking is not enough—the role-play experience can aid the learning many-fold.

IMPLEMENTATION: Use of role-play with couples was focused on in T.I.P. #68. Role-play also works well in individual treatment, especially with the anxious client or one who wants to be able to act more assertively instead of aggressively or non-assertively. An example that comes to mind is a client who was fearful of a family party at his house over the weekend. After discussing what he was anxious about to no avail, we role-played how he would act with a chosen aunt. It became apparent why he was so nervous! He was not using "party talk!" I then had him play the aunt and I played him exactly as he spoke; he was appalled at how bad he sounded, as he just droned on and on about his anxiety problem. I then role modeled a better way to react to the aunt's concern about his "anxiety problem," and then he tried it again more successfully. The next week he reported that he had had a great time at the party and was only minimally nervous, and felt that the behavioral rehearsal gave him a lot of confidence in knowing how to expect the unexpected.

PROCESSING: The use of role-play has unlimited potential and has proved effective in giving clients a sense of hands-on rehearsal and knowledge for how to manage communication and anxiety.

T.I.P. #84
THE POWER OF BIBLIOTHERAPY

THEORY: Bibliotherapy often provides greatly needed assistance when working with clients. I strongly believe the role of the clinician is to be knowledgeable about what literature clients can use as resources to help them in particular situations. I have found it helpful to keep a list of resources to recommend. Through bibliotherapy, clients can continue the therapeutic process between sessions on their own.

IMPLEMENTATION: The following page is a sampling of titles I use for a few topics that relate to many of my clients. Clients often ask me to recommended books; I have made it a priority to know what is out there to help clients become increasingly knowledgeable and empowered. I sometimes order extra copies of some common titles and popular topics from Amazon to have on hand to lend to clients, as some of the lightly used books cost just a few dollars.

PROCESSING: Bibliotherapy is a powerful tool that should not be underestimated. Clients often feel relieved to have tangible hands-on help in the form of a book. Choosing relevant material takes some research on the therapist's part. As an example, the following page has some recommendations for the individual who is either the legacy, co-dependent, or loved one of an individual with Borderline or Narcissistic Personality Disorder.

SAMPLE BIBLIOTHERAPY TOPIC:
DEALING WITH NARCISSISTIC OR BORDERLINE PERSONALITIES

Bibliotherapy:

Read Two Books and Let's Talk Next Week: Using Bibliotherapy in Clinical Practice
—Joshua and DiMenna

Books Dealing with Narcissism:

Why Is It Always About You? Saving Yourself from Narcissists in Your Life
—Sandy Hotchkiss

Children of the Self-Absorbed: A Grown-Up's Guide to Getting Over Narcissistic Parents
—Nina Brown

Working with the Self-Absorbed: How to Handle Narcissistic Personalities on the Job
—Nina Brown

The Wizard of Oz and Other Narcissists
—Eleanor Payson

Identifying and Understanding the Narcissistic Personality
—Elsa F. Ronningstam

Books Dealing with Borderline Personality:

Surviving a Borderline Parent: How to Heal Your Childhood Wounds and Build Trust, Boundaries and Self-Esteem
—Kimberlee Roth

Stop Walking on Eggshells
—Mason and Kreger

Stop Walking on Eggshells Workbook
—Kreger & Shirley

Emotional Vampires: Dealing with People Who Drain You Dry
—Bernstein

Borderline Personality Disorder Demystified: An Essential Guide to Understanding and Living with BPD
—Robert Friedel et al.

T.I.P. #85
THE POWER OF CARTOON THERAPY

THEORY: Using a variety of cartoons is a fun, creative, and humorous way to learn and understand many "life skills." Through laughter and lightness, clients learn to incorporate serious principles into their lives. They can learn to appreciate topics concerning the importance of self-esteem, rational thinking, communication, how to diffuse anger, and how to look on the bright side of disappointment.

Humor helps relieve stress and reminds one not to take oneself so seriously. Humor is an important stress buster. Humor has been linked to overcoming serious illness and to illness prevention.

IMPLEMENTATION: Explain to your client that by using humor to overcome resistance to change, cartoon intervention becomes serious stuff! As the late "Peanuts" creator Charles Schultz so aptly put, "If I could give a gift to the next generation, it would be the ability for each individual to laugh at himself." Because stress relief can be achieved through humor, I enjoy enlarging and copying cartoons and using them with clients in my office or in groups or workplace wellness workshops through Power Point. Books by psychiatrist Abraham Twerski are excellent demonstrations of the power of humor through use of "Peanuts" cartoons as therapeutic insight into self-esteem. Two of these books that stand out are *"When Do the Good Things Start?"* and *"Life's Too Short."*

PROCESSING: Whatever vehicle you use—whether it be placing a book of therapeutic cartoons in your waiting room or recommending books such as Twerski's—humor can go a long way to enlighten clients on the importance of seeing the lighter side of life. How much do anxiety and worry interfere with our functioning—anxiety and worry often over things that might never even happen in real life! As Winston Churchill said, "When I look back on all these worries, I remember the story of the old man who said on his deathbed that he had had a lot of trouble in his life, most of which had never happened!"

T.I.P. #86
THE POWER OF CINEMATHERAPY

THEORY: Like with Bibliotherapy, Cinematherapy has provided me with powerful tools for working with both individuals and groups. Relating to those in movies can be powerful in understanding oneself.

IMPLEMENTATION: In individual therapy, I might suggest a movie that relates to the individual, and ask him/her to rent and watch it, and then we can discuss it. In a group situation, including workplace wellness groups or mental health in-service training groups, I provide video clips to show important therapeutic principles. Another option would be to show an entire movie and discuss it over a few weeks' time, depending on the timing of the group. There are many ways to use movies. My favorite movie depicting psychological issues is *Ordinary People.* In this movie, one can recognize themes relating to personality disorders, depression, suicidal behavior, unhealthy coping skills, co-dependency, forgiveness, communication, hope, and healing—all in one powerful movie! Here are a few books that you can use as resources to find movies that fit in with your treatment goal:

> *Reel People: Finding Ourselves in the Movies*—Gluss
>
> *Rent Two Films and Let's Talk in the Morning*—Hesley
>
> *Reel Psychiatry: Movie Portrayals of Psychiatric Conditions*—Robinson
>
> *Movies & Mental Illness*—Wedding

PROCESSING: Cinematherapy has an advantage over more traditional therapy in that one can experience and visualize concepts through memorable media. The power of movies is unlimited in its potential.

AFTERWORD

Hopefully there have been some T.I.P.S. included here that you have begun to use already with your clients. I know that many of you reading this workbook have also used your own ideas and tools that have been successful in treatment for either individuals or groups. I invite you to share them in my future book that will be entitled, *The Therapeutic Collaborative Workbook,* which will feature "Greatest Hits" in creative treatment approaches. If you would be interested in sharing your ideas, please submit them to JABelmont@worksiteinsights.com.

All references will be cited and credit given on the printed feature. For more information, please contact me for submission requirements.

Judith Belmont, M.S.
2006